Patterns of Faith

Patterns of Faith

A study in the relationship between the
New Testament and Christian doctrine

J. L. HOULDEN

FORTRESS PRESS
Philadelphia

In grateful memory of Austin Farrer

© 1977 SCM Press Ltd, London

Library of Congress Catalog Card Number 76-55829
ISBN 0-8006-0493-8

Printed in Great Britain   1-493

Contents

Everything bends
    to re-enact
        the poem lived,
        lived not written,
    the poem spoken
    by Christ, who never
wrote a word,
    saboteur
        of received ideas
            who rebuilt Rome
                with the words he
            never wrote;
        whether sacred,
    whether human,
himself a sunrise
    of love enlarged;
        of love, enlarged.*

* From William Plomer, 'A Church in Bavaria', in *Celebrations*, Jonathan Cape 1972 and reproduced by kind permission of the Estate of William Plomer.

Preface

This book may raise a little dust for some of its readers. That would be a pity; for it is a *ballon d'essai*, a shot at a target. It is in many ways rough and sketchy. But it seeks to generate not alarm but hope. The object of attention is the deepest roots of Christian belief, in the very first moments when it came to birth. But the standpoint is within our society in our day and the intention is to walk with freedom in the streets of its culture. It shies away from mental ghettoes, and perhaps its deepest conviction is that God himself does not like them very much. Theology does not always do him the honour of sharing this preference. Indeed it is a commentary on much of what follows that if theology and its protectors were not in our society deprived of teeth (whether out of indifference or, more commendably, a belief in tolerance) a book like this, by a minor but devoted practitioner, might not have had the confidence and the freedom to contribute to the enterprise. The book is not primarily an apologia for Christian belief. Its aim is simply to explore the fundamental geography of the Christian land, to aid understanding and ease certain difficulties for Christians and others. But understanding may renew love and kindle acceptance; and that would be, from every point of view, healthy. It is unhealthy that theology has so largely lost the power to bear directly on the realities of life, having interposed a conceptual (and institutional) jungle. Any attempt to make a garden of it can almost demand applause!

I am grateful to Dennis Nineham of Keble College, Oxford, and Alan Race, assistant curate of Tupsley, Hereford, who read what I wrote, made helpful suggestions and voiced healthy doubts; and to friends and pupils who worked for this book without realizing it; and to Peter Strange, assistant curate of St John's Church, Newcastle-upon-Tyne, who read the proofs.

I

Brethren at Variance

'Theology' now covers so many distinct and diverse areas of enquiry that the word easily confuses. A man may expect one kind of article and be served with another. As he sets out on theological study, he may hope to receive answers to questions about the existence and being of God and be told instead only how those questions were answered in the second or sixteenth century. He was seeking doctrinal reasoning, he was given a piece of history. 'Theology' means studies that are linguistic, historical, philosophical, and some that are odd, ill-defined mixtures of all three. People calling themselves theologians may find themselves at home in circles as different as those of oriental linguists and linguistic philosophers. A student may emerge from an undergraduate course in theology in one university quite incapable of coherent discourse on matters which many would suppose to be the heart of the subject – like reasons for belief in God, the value and function of the Bible, or the place of Christianity alongside other world religions. He may, however, know what the biblical texts meant in their original setting and be able to say what leading Christians of the fourth century taught. In another university, it will be quite the reverse – haziness on the texts and the history, coherence in abstract argument. And the one may well despise the other.

This diversity has its benefits. It is in any case the natural result of specialization. The branches of any subject rapidly develop their own ways of working, their own language, and their own corporate identity. Without it, knowledge would not grow. But there is a price to pay. Types of study commonly develop by grazing in the connected fields. For example, a philosophical theologian will find his work becoming fruitful as he shares in the general intellectual discipline of philosophy, in which he will meet not only 'pure' philosophers but also others who began from other centres, like philosophers of science. The price paid is often a growing estrangement between one aspect of the parent discipline of study and another. Whether this matters or not depends upon the continuing vitality of the parent. In some circumstances it may outlive its usefulness and no harm will come if it is allowed to die. Whether rightly or wrongly, people do not now fight hard to keep the independent study of English grammar alive, in the style which once dominated the classroom; instead, the benefits are (sometimes) acquired through literary or linguistic studies.

In the case of theology, the threat to the parent has gone almost unnoticed. And it is not entirely clear what kind of threat exists. Perhaps it is a case of slow death by dismemberment. Dismemberment of a peculiarly hubristic brand: for the possessor of each part sometimes believes that what he holds is as good as the whole. Thus, there are biblical scholars who write as if the results of their studies *were* Christian theology; and even when (as usually) there is no explicit claim, the distinctness of the discipline makes it implicit. I have written elsewhere about the case of liturgical study, where the growth of the subject, reaching out in this case into the field of historical studies, has brought its own professionalism – an admirable result, until tasks arise, such as the provision of new forms of service, where the contributions of other aspects of theological study could with advantage be used but in practice are neglected.[1] Sometimes the results may be interesting for our present purpose, as an example will show.

In an examination, candidates were asked to write on 'the theology of' the Third Series Communion Service of the Church of England, and the intention was evidently that they should comment on its doctrinal content and implications. I intend no disparagement of my colleagues if, as one of those responsible for drawing up that service, I report that, in the sense intended, doctrinal considerations played only a minimal part in its formation. It was constructed on liturgical not doctrinal principles, that is from within the territory of liturgical studies, both in its historical and more pragmatic aspects. If examination candidates then discover a 'theology' within it, they have found something which exists independently of the conscious action of its writers, an achievement not impossible but worth remarking.

Liturgy (for example) thus goes its own way, decreasingly aware of belonging to a wider whole and of being only part heir of a richer inheritance. Worse still, not only has liturgical study become less capable, because of its own independent development, of ranging beyond the purely liturgical field, even when its tasks may be thought to demand it, but it shows little awareness that such wider resources might be clamouring to be used. It is not hard to show that modern liturgy-making often betrays an innocence of the biblical study of the past century and of trends in doctrinal thinking during the modern period which perfectly illustrates this academic parochialism. (For examples, see the article referred to in note 1 above.)

But has the atomizing of theological studies, of which this is one example, really gone so far that the parent 'theology' is now more notional than identifiable? And does the term cover so many kinds of study that it is now too broad to be useful? Are we anywhere near the position of having as many concepts of the subject, as many ways of approaching it, as we have theologians?

Certainly not at the level of the expectations of the Christian community. However nebulous it may be, there is an area of discussion and statement called 'theological'. The ground may be approached from various starting-points (whether the Bible, or tradition, or official ecclesiastical statements), but its existence cannot be doubted. It corresponds most closely to that aspect or department of formal theological enquiry labelled 'dogmatic theology' or 'systematic theology': that is, concern with the rationale and implications of belief in God according to the Christian pattern.

The subject of this book is the relationship between that central theological area, Christian doctrine, and perhaps its closest associate within the range of theological subjects, New Testament studies. It is the most intricate and far-reaching example of the phenomena whose outlines we have drawn. The relationship between liturgical studies, as they branch out and form their own identity, and other theological areas may have more immediate implications for everyday church life (its effects are on display every Sunday), but when it comes to the understanding and formulation of Christian truth, clearly the case now before us is crucial. Yet how little attention it receives! After a centuries-long tradition in which the New Testament was used, with comparatively little sophistication, partly as the source and partly as the backing of doctrinal statement, New Testament studies began to develop their own autonomous identity. With the rise of historical criticism, they acquired affiliations with other branches of study and formed their own criteria of objective scholarship. There is no need to do more than list a few of those affinities: with textual criticism, archaeology, literary analysis of various kinds, and the religious thought of the world contemporary with the New Testament writings. While there have been from time to time strident war-cries to

3

the effect that New Testament scholarship is subversive of orthodox faith, there has been a strange lack of sustained and thoughtful analysis of the relationship which might now be proper between these studies of the New Testament and the formulation of Christian belief. As the study of the New Testament has become increasingly a formal entity, so the two areas of discussion (both standing under the umbrella of 'theology') have in practice shown reluctance to interact in a spirit of genuine understanding of each other's accomplishments. Yet on the face of it, they cannot for a moment exist apart and should be in perpetual dance with each other. For Christian affirmation is indissolubly concerned with words and events and persons for which essential evidence is in the New Testament, and those events and persons demand interpretation which does justice to what can be known about them.

The two disciplines have gone their separate ways, to the detriment of both. On the side of New Testament studies, much of the work is of course technical and innocent of immediate doctrinal connections. But once the New Testament scholar removes himself even a little from the detailed material and begins to take an overall view of the documents, it is remarkable how doctrinally naive he can often be.

At this level, we single out two pervasive ills: anachronism and harmonizing. How often have New Testament scholars approached the New Testament with the doctrinal agenda of later Christianity in their minds – an agenda formed by creeds and other authoritative church formulations? There is an undeclared assumption that somehow that pattern of belief lurks in the documents, waiting to be uncovered. Of course its expression was at that early stage rudimentary and imprecise by later standards, of course the idiom of expression found in the New Testament did not always persist when the gospel found itself in alien soil, but still the essential doctrinal pattern was constant. Harmonizing too; essentially, the New Testament church spoke with one voice. There might indeed be differences of emphasis, variations within the formulation of the early proclamation, but they may without difficulty be subsumed into unity. This happy result tends to be achieved by organizing the conceptual appreciation of the New Testament around one dominant figure, generally Paul or John, and letting the distinctive voices of the rest fade into a harmonious background chorus. Or else around a theological theme discernible in the New Testament or plausibly to be derived from it – or rather, once more, from some part of it. Thus 'salvation history' has played such a role for a whole wave of scholars as they

4

have sought to present their broad conclusions in digestible form: but how doubtful it is whether such a concept, as commonly presented, is prominent in writings other than those of Luke and perhaps the Epistle to the Hebrews. As far as the rest are concerned, this phrase, nowhere found in the New Testament itself, scarcely springs to mind as the most obvious way of describing their doctrinal heart. Similarly, it is well recognized that the existentialist interpretation of Christian faith associated with the teaching of Rudolf Bultmann can be seen more readily as a modern restatement of the thought of Paul than of any other writer represented in the New Testament. Even then, the justice of the restatement is highly contestable on the grounds of anachronism. The ancient writer is being viewed through the eyes of a modern philosophical position, which, however striking its similarities to the earlier doctrine, is in many ways poles apart from it.

If New Testament scholars are often inclined, when they venture into the doctrinal field, to oversimplify or falsify in ways such as these, restatements of Christian doctrine equally often use the New Testament in ways which betray a clumsy appreciation of the work which has been expended upon it in the past century and more. Sometimes the doctrinal writer works so close to the New Testament that his operations shade into some of those undertaken by New Testament scholars. As we have seen, major formulations of Christian doctrine have in recent years sometimes been gathered round a single great theme, grounded in the New Testament, and the work of Bultmann could be evaluated from this point of view at least as suitably as from the side of New Testament studies. More clearly doctrinally based examples are the work of Wolfhart Pannenberg, focusing on the theme of resurrection,[2] and Jürgen Moltmann, centering on the Christian hope.[3] In cases such as these, the New Testament scholar must record that there has been a major streamlining of the New Testament evidence, a determined elimination of the rich diversity of viewpoint there represented – as indeed the very fact that quite different themes can be selected as *the* theme by different scholars indicates. The truth is that while the theme concerned certainly finds a prominent place in the New Testament documents, it has (however assiduous the reference to New Testament texts) been abstracted from its setting, erected into independent existence, and, within a modern context of thought, treated as a base from which to formulate the traditional programme of Christian doctrine. That programme is usually taken as 'given' and not as something which itself merits criticism. Even where it is radically reinterpreted (as for example with regard to the resurrection in the case of Bultmann, where the traditional historical grounding of that doctrine is denied), a feeling tends to persist that the items or headings of the conventional programme should remain. The implications, that the programme has a timeless validity, that the enterprise of Christian theology is bound to it for ever, and that, whatever the degree and nature of development sustained by Christian doctrine, it can never be remoulded, demand careful examination.

It is the case then that, despite the appearance given by certain writers (e.g. Pannenberg's *Jesus, God and Man* with its array of New Testament references), the two disciplines of critical New Testament studies and dogmatic theology have increasingly moved apart. Each has its own methods and conventions. Much of the work in each field is carried out in effective oblivion of the other, to the degree sometimes of extreme naivety concerning one another's achievements and challenges. And where there appears to be interaction, the principles on which it rests often, on examination, do violence to the subtlety of the New Testament evidence or fail to do justice to the doctrinal questions which, in the modern context (which includes the results of biblical scholarship) present themselves. The New Testament scholar sometimes behaves as if he had made satisfying doctrinal statements by repeating the thought of (some part of) the New Testament in current idiom; the doctrinal theologian as if he had grounded his work in the New Testament by referring to apparently apposite passages at suitable points in his independently based flow of thought.

May the theological enterprise as a whole not profit from the sharp questions which each has to ask the other? Do such questions not impose themselves? Thus, New Testament scholarship has come to recognize certain major factors which colour its whole work. The writings are seen as the fruit of early Christian community life, determined by its interests, arising from its needs, and formed by the pressures to which it was subject. The historical settings from which the writings come and to which they bear witness are before the mind, so that they are read (from the point of view of New Testament studies) not with an eye to the long tradition of Christian thought and writing which lay ahead of them, but as examples of religious writing of the eastern Mediterranean in the first century and early second century. There is a recognition of the diversity of thought and formulation within the early Christian congregations and the accidental quality (historically speaking) of the material which has survived, so that we cannot tell how far the picture given by the New Testament, dominated as it is by the writings of Paul and his Pauline successors, is an accurate and balanced portrayal of the state of affairs in the church of the period. And it is not forgotten that the New Testament we possess reflects not only the life and thought of the earliest Christian generations, which it has always been seen as illuminating, but also the interests of Christians in the quite lengthy period during which the writings were being collected and receiving authoritative status, i.e. turned into 'the New Testament'.

These considerations pose searching questions for the Christian dogmatic theologian. Here are some of them. Is it early Christian thought or the thought of the New Testament which may be thought to have special importance for Christian doctrine? If the former, can we be sure we know enough about it? If the latter, what view of the New Testament as canonical scripture must then be presupposed? How far is it possible, given the diversity of theological patterns among the various New Testament writers, to extract a single pattern sufficiently coherent and comprehensive to serve as the basis for any modern attempt to reach a unified statement of doctrine or even as the first stage in the evolution of a homogeneous body of Christian doctrine in the early church? What is the status of Christian formulations of the first century, which are expressed in the thought forms of the period and arise from assumptions valid in a culture long since forsaken, when it comes to the present-day statement of Christian belief? How may the gap between the two be evaluated? It is bridged by long centuries of Christian use of many of the terms concerned but that use was largely unaware of the contrasts of culture and mental outlook now so clear to us. With what eyes then may we view the ancient but so persistent text? What difference should it make to the agenda of doctrinal statement when serious questions about the nature of alleged historical 'facts' impose themselves? That is, what happens to traditional doctrinal headings such as 'resurrection', 'ascension', 'Holy Spirit' when historical foundations, long taken for granted, are open to question? What is the status of the whole endeavour called christology in view of the obscurity which envelops the figure of Jesus, who is visible only through the medium of texts witnessing indirectly to him? Along these lines, the very existence of modern New Testament scholarship interrogates anyone attempting the task of formulating Christian doctrine.

The doctrinal theologian also has questions to pose to the New

Testament scholar – not in the more scientific aspects of his work, but when he turns to derive overall conclusions from it. He will question, for example, his common assumption that once it has be⸻ understood, the New Testament church (or such part of it as fin expression in the writings which survive to us) has 'something to s to us, or at any rate wish to elucidate the sense in which that cont tion may be taken. He will also ask what it means to 'understand' ancient text – and what it means to stand in the same tradition w those from whom the text arose, a tradition which it has done much to form. He may be interested to discover what, if anything special about these texts within the religious and cultural envir ment which produced them. What forces led to their emergence: what respects do they deserve the weight which has been pla upon them and to what degree is that the result of later pressur

In the nature of the case, it is the doctrinal task which comes ir the sharper interrogation, and the New Testament scholar ch ly exposes himself to questions when he departs from his scholarly ⸻ef and sets up as a provider of doctrine or when he turns to the w ⸻er implications of his technical work.

In all that has been said, we have accepted the departmentali ng which has increasingly characterized theological (like other) stu es in the modern period. As we have seen, certain benefits may ⸻ se from working with that departmental model – though the conten ⸻n is that the reaping of them has been comparatively feeble. Rat ⸻r, their distinctness has been accepted and each has more and n re gone its own way. But a unified model of 'the theological enterp e' may in the end be more profitable and less artificial for achie ⸻g certain desirable objectives. There is after all no clear reason y theology should eternally organize itself exclusively in its traditi al departments, particularly if, as seems to be the case, they lack e capacity to interact fruitfully – as a result of the sheer force of e specialization each demands of its practitioners. But the uni d model here envisaged is in no sense a return, born of nostalgia, to e days before the rise of specialization. There is no intention to ab don or even to blur the distinctive demands and achievements of, example, New Testament scholarship. But there is a plea that th engaged in the theological enterprise should evaluate their task afre and be ready to lay their hands without inhibition or a sense academic protocol upon any evidence and techniques that are ge mane to their purposes. They should not be constrained by convei tions of theological scholarship which may have been rendere obsolete by that evidence or those techniques. For example, if the traditional division of Christian doctrine into a series of topics, ...rived from an overall view of scripture and formed by the creeds ...d other summaries of Christian faith, is called in question by the ...ident results of the critical study of Christian origins from which ...me of those topics were ultimately derived, then that manner of ...nceptualizing Christian belief had better be abandoned as obsolete ...d other arrangements adopted, more fitting to the new circum- ...nces. There is sometimes a tendency to envisage the possibility of ...ne such shift of perspective in some of the traditional areas but to ...ard others, equally part of the conventional scheme and arrived at ...exactly the same way, as sacrosanct: without *this* belief left distinct ...l intact, it is alleged, Christian faith is being shipwrecked. So, for ...mple: let it be admitted that the ascension of Christ is a subordin- ...doctrine, based in scripture only upon the particular manner of ...ological story-telling favoured by Luke; it is a different matter ...n resurrection and incarnation – these are inviolate areas in which ...writ of tradition runs eternally. We may leave aside the merits of ...se examples, and agree that to draw the line in such a manner is to ...ibit the total process of restatement. It is indeed more serious still: ...such a procedure will make any restatement lopsided and superfi- .... Success is bound to depend upon freedom to view the field of ...istian theology as a whole. It cannot be satisfactory to leave ...laves where the inhabitants wear the costumes and favour the ...ners of a former era – and then to regard those enclaves as key ...nts in the country to which special deference is due. One might as ...l interpret the world of London fashions from a standpoint which ...egarded the Chelsea pensioners as the norm.

So an important effect of the adoption of a unified model is likely to be alteration in the traditional doctrinal agenda. Free intercourse ...h biblical study ought to have this effect, for even if scripture is ...wed quite conservatively, the facts that it is more flexible concep- ...lly, and that it antedates the schematizing of doctrine, will ... oduce a degree of loosening. And while many of the questions to which an answer may be sought from New Testament scholarship remain (and probably will always remain) without assured results, nevertheless the obstinate presence of many of its major perspectives and assumptions (such as those listed above, see p. 7) means that other less objective, more speculative areas of theological study (such as the formulation of doctrine) are bound to be swayed by it, once they enter into serious interaction with it.

The dominant characteristic of a unified model for the Christian theological enterprise is then likely to be some form of interplay between the concerns broadly belonging to the study of the New Testament and those belonging to the study of doctrine. Here is the central platform on which Christian theology works out its debates, and all other areas of theological study (whether the Old Testament, philosophy of religion, liturgy, or the comparative study of religions) subserve it.

The aim of this study is to examine frankly the conditions of that interplay. 'Frankly' because, as will be clear, it seems at present to be at a stage where maturity is resisted. If the two parties, so intimately related, so clearly meant for mutual enrichment, do not live in isolation from each other, then certainly they frequently show little awareness of each other's workings and little desire to pool resources. Yet how can either live in health without the other? Christian doctrine, so heavily undergirded in all its traditional assumptions and vocabulary by its historical origins, with regard to both ideas and events, cannot subsist on sketchy or outdated acquaintance with New Testament realities. Even if the conclusions of New Testament scholarship are, like other kinds of scholarship, to some degree ephemeral and subject to fashion, the remedy can never be to rest content with one particular stage in its development, as if it embodied the final truth of the matter. Similarly, those who investigate the New Testament must not limit their appreciation of what they find there to the requirements and interests of some limited conception of Christian theological needs. Christian theology must adapt itself – in both expression and content (and who may decide in advance where the line lies between the two?) – to what is shown to be true concerning Christian origins, in so far as they affect it. The degree to which Christian origins bear on doctrine is not a matter to be decided too readily; it is itself one of the prime questions implicit in the interplay with which we are concerned. If all this means a certain mobility in the statement of Christian doctrine, then that too is no matter for regret. It is an inevitable feature of a faith which is at certain points open to historical investigation and seeks always to express itself in relation to whatever in human thought and experience is valuable and relevant to its concerns. Christian theism bears that character and carries that risk.

In this book we shall proceed by making soundings of different kinds. Each will begin from some aspect of the New Testament and will aim to discover the doctrinal implications of the topic investigated. We shall try to see, for example, what, in their own terms, was the shape of the belief of some of the leading New Testament writers, subject as they were to no central unifying direction with regard to their conceptual structure, and in most cases unaware, as far as we can see, of responsibility to toe allotted lines; but rather compelled by circumstance to create new forms of thought and to speculate afresh in the endeavour to make sense of dramatic and forceful religious experience. We shall also examine certain major doctrinal concerns and see how they fared at the hands of various individuals and groups represented in the New Testament writings. These soundings will lead us to the position where we are compelled to evaluate afresh the function and nature of Christian doctrinal statement. We shall be able to take a fresh view of what may and what may not be affirmed; what is demanded and what is rendered obsolete or redundant. But these useful results will only follow when New Testament and doctrinal interests are allowed to enter into unrestrained and unconditional intimacy – in the interests of the total enterprise, which never loses its pristine aim, to clothe in words the precious Christian experience of God.

II

Theological Progress

Before we embark on the programme outlined at the end of the last chapter, it will aid clarity if we attempt to elucidate the remoter background from which the task is undertaken. Though much of the analysis provided above is the merest commonsense and quite uncontroversial, other factors affecting the viewpoint to be adopted in this study are less matters of consensus. Some of them do not come into the open as easily as they should, others are familiar; some, once attention is drawn to them, are scarcely deniable, others are liable to meet vigorous opposition. We have already rooted ourselves in current theological activities. We continue to do so, but from a different angle. It concerns a familiar aspect of the present theological scene.

'Theologians', said a French priest to me impatiently, 'are the technicians of the divisions of the church.' For him, looking at the church with that generous ecumenical spirit so typical of large parts of European Catholicism in recent years, 'theology' meant hairsplitting, losing sight of the gospel in the interests of intellectual and traditional correctness. Its practitioners maintained the machinery they had been set to mind, but had no talent for creative work. In England, many practical Christians find some theologians equally objectionable – but for almost exactly the opposite reason. Far from perpetuating stale controversy with other Christians by their pernickety ways, they move so far from traditional Christian positions that they seem to be abandoning all the old fixed landmarks, long seen as defining the bounds of recognizably orthodox faith. Soaring, adventurous thought (or, if you prefer it, reckless, undisciplined thought) threatens to cut loose from familiar moorings and to drift off towards featureless, unmapped and unmappable heavens.

We repeat – there is nothing novel about that: it has been a recurring theme, as far as English church history is concerned, at least since the publication of *Essays and Reviews* in 1860. Nor is it at all surprising. If university theologians, paid to think, did not think thoughts unthought by clergymen too occupied in pastoral life to read many books and by lay persons relatively unskilled in the subject, then they would merit dismissal. Who ever attacked a professor of physics for violating the orthodoxy he had learnt at school or in a first degree course in the subject thirty years ago? Certainly one might attack him if he did *not*.

Surely, it will be objected, the cases are not equivalent. All disciplines of study do not bear the same character. Physics marches on as fresh observation of the universe takes place and more refined hypotheses are advanced to account for what is observed. But how can theology *march on*? Clearly it can, as we have seen, in its historical aspects – in all that derives from its being concerned with matters rooted in a long and rich past and not springing *de novo* from this morning's spontaneous speculation about the deep riddles of life. But it is surely a different matter as far as its more theoretical and speculative aspects are concerned. In the case of *Christian* theology, however, can the two be distinguished? It has been commonly thought that, at least in part, they can. It is not difficult to feel that doctrinal structures and patterns of belief have a durability denied, in theory at least, to that which is open to historical investigation and possible falsification. And even a man who is sceptical of traditional patterns may feel that present doctrinal formulations are unaffected by the growth of historical knowledge concerning fourth-century Alexandrian or eighteenth-century German theological thought.

But go back a little further, and the case is less clear. Will the doctrinal structure, the pattern of my belief, remain unaffected by increased knowledge, any conceivable increased knowledge, of the first-century church, or of Jesus himself? Is Christian theology not inescapably a matter of reaction to historical events and circumstances concerning which more information does from time to time become available and may continue to do so?

Further, even if that did not occur, the perspective must necessarily change, in relation to both the historical data and the apparently so durable structure of thought and belief. So at this point at any rate Christian theology has a fluidity and vulnerability which make it possible to talk of movement sufficiently analogous to that in physics. It cannot avoid being of such a character that its theoretical structure may be forced to 'give' in the light of fresh historical knowledge and changes in intellectual perspective.

13

Knowledge of the history of Christianity, in particular its origins, may advance and in certain cases that may, in theory at least, have doctrinal consequences. But the growth of acquired information is only part of the story. Let us look further at the question of 'shifts in perspective' to which we have just referred.

The ninth-century Welsh historian Nennius announced that he wrote his history of Britain simply by making a heap of all the information he could find – and thereby showed himself naive (though pardonably so) about his own work. There is the accumulation of knowledge; there is also the taking up of a point of view and the sifting of it in the light of particular and changing considerations and pressures, factors felt to be significant. Even in areas where the state of knowledge is relatively static (as in some areas of biblical studies), changes in viewpoint arise and impose themselves, with serious consequences, potentially at least, not only for the view to be taken of the past itself but also for more theoretical structures such as doctrinal patterns. It is not so much that existing belief is then eroded or denied as that it changes shape when seen from the fresh standpoint – and cannot now be seen otherwise. Features and formulations formerly seen as compelling fade from sight and it even becomes hard to imagine why they once seemed so powerful and clear.[4] Doctrine develops less by gradual growth (comparable to that of a living organism) than by changes of shape and direction whose complexity defies the application of simple imagery. When the theologian, paid to think, finds himself in the van (where else should he be?) of such development, it is not surprising that he sometimes astonishes and shocks those who follow. To be the antennae of the Christian body has its risks (including that of making unprofitable probes), but it also has the chance to make freshly appropriate statements of Christian faith. But how are we to tell what is appropriate? To that question we shall return. Meanwhile we shall retrace our steps.

We noted a distinction between increase in knowledge of eighteenth-century German or fourth-century Alexandrian theology and increase in knowledge of theology in the primitive church and of the person and teaching of Jesus. The former might be supposed to leave the present doctrinal structure of the Christian faith unaffected and serve merely to widen understanding of Christian history and, doubtless, to deepen appreciation of present Christian teaching and belief. But the latter is bound to have more important effects for it is concerned with the events to which the Christian faith is the

14

response and reaction and of which Christian doctrine seeks to give verbal explication. But is the distinction so neat and complete? Leaving aside for the moment Jesus himself, is not Christian theology in every period, from the earliest to the most recent, on the same footing in this respect, that it is the reaction, expressed in a particular pattern of thought and in a particular cultural setting, to *that which presented itself* – namely, Jesus and that which derived from him? It is this last element – 'that which derived from him' – which takes us inexorably into the realm of the relative, the culturally conditioned. Even if we can begin by seeing the figure of Jesus as in a certain sense 'given' – simply placed before us – his words, his every gesture, arouse a response which is different for each observer and formed by the whole complex self which is brought to that moment. And what is true of response to the speech and action of Jesus in the case of those who experienced them directly is true with increasing complexity of all others who experience 'him' through the activities and words of the church, which in both content and setting shift and stir incessantly.

Yet the fact of cultural change ought not to induce vertiginous horror in face of an apparently infinite complexity. A theologian setting about his task in, for example, the seventeenth century does not simply place a little more material on top of a pile whose contents and composition he has painstakingly examined and grasped. Even if he claims to be doing no more than restating what his fathers have held and wishes to assert no originality, his debt will be, albeit unconsciously, at least as great to the movements of thought and sensibility, the priorities of concern, in the society around him, as to the past which is the avowed object of his loyalty. In that respect his contribution is as fresh and original as that of the apostle Paul, the first known practitioner of the craft. From this point of view, he stands not on the shoulders of Paul (and the rest, as in some huge gymnastic pyramid), but in a circle with him, looking inwards at that from which both derive.

Looking inwards at the same object, yes: but because of their different standpoints and settings, seeing something different. And then making, inevitably, a different verbal formulation, or if the same formulation then with new meaning, new tone, new emphasis. It is the case not only with theologians working within an articulate and observable tradition, but also at the less rigorous level of the ordinary thinking believer. He too may be brought within the category of 'theologian' in so far as he brings his faith to coherent verbal expression and makes of it something other than a movement of the heart. Put it thus: if a sensitive enough instrument could be devised, every reciter of the creed could be shown to be meaning something different by it, however strenuously he affirmed his solidarity with the Christian past and present; and, in accordance with the degree of intellectual vigour, every occasion of recitation could be made to register its own small variation of sense or shade of emphasis.

Such is the condition of Christian theology, in common with all other human intellectual enterprises. Alongside it we place the myth of permanence and identity, enshrined in the Vincentian Canon – that catholic orthodoxy consists of that which has been believed everywhere, always, and by all – and intensified by every person, every rite, every institution which gives a sense of the age-long durability of the Christian faith. The very fact that it can now be seen (at least by some) as a myth is of course itself a message conveyed by the antennae, certainly not absorbed by the body as a whole; a message received from certain features of the surrounding cultural atmosphere. Sensitivity to the depth and width of historical change – of its extension into the areas of thought-patterns and of what is deemed credible, so that one generation's assumptions are another's superstitions or curiosities; awareness of the complexity of historical causation and of the interlocking quality, at different levels, of all human action, so that the idea of the persistence of insulated threads of intellectual development becomes incredible; awareness of cultural coherence, so that certain features of thought come to seem out of tune with the dominant patterns by which people live at a particular time and place; these are so much part of many people's consciousness – and show every sign of spreading – that their profound effects on Christian theology had better be reckoned with before they occasion yet another of those episodes of outrage and panic which have assaulted and humiliated the church since the days of Buckland and Darwin. Indeed, whereas a few years ago the most significant intellectual distinctions among Christians had already moved from those determined by confession or denomination to those between 'conservatives' and 'progressives' or 'radicals', it is becoming more and more accurate now to place them between those who have become more aware of the overarching fact of historical relativity and those who have not. Once the new consciousness has dawned, it is not (we repeat) so much a matter of old beliefs being eroded or abandoned, not a matter of betrayal of a static, rocklike faith, as of belief taking on new shapes, fresh proportions, being seen in a new light, so that the old loses force rather than 'truth' and new patterns simply emerge to carry conviction.

Nevertheless, not only the restraining (and romantic?) force of piety but also knowledge and common sense forbid certain kinds of exaggeration. Let us admit freely that there are great differences between the theology of Paul and that of his innumerable successors, even those who reckoned to do no more than re-present his thought. Yet they all witness to what is recognizably the same faith. Especially when viewed from outside, all belong within a single world of discourse, however different their idiom and emphasis. Of course Aquinas, for example, moved in an intellectual setting vastly different from ours, but we can still follow, admire and share his work and allow it to build up ours. And the very sensitive instrument which would disclose the differences between the intentions of our apparently so uniform creed-reciters would also reveal how close they were to each other. Much depends, clearly, on the object selected for attention, whether the unity or the diversity. But which of these is chiefly noticed is itself a matter of cultural conditioning. Through most of its history, Christian theology has worked in an atmosphere which has given the highest value to continuity and uniformity. The effort has gone into providing stability, finding (and often enforcing) unity of statement, reckoning diversity a weakness and a source of confusion. Intellectual endeavour has most often taken expressions of belief as given and devoted itself only to their explication. The task of elucidation and formulation has involved no movement from a known base, only the illumination of its shape and colour. Controversy has arisen not from deliberate new departures demanded by recognized new circumstances but from attempts to interpret the old with greater authenticity.

Effort so applied is now, to say the least, unfashionable; for many, it is unthinkable, impossible. The 'known base' is now not so much a body of identifiable propositions or statements of belief as a style of 'sound' intellectual method; primary loyalty goes to intellectual integrity. Then the task is to analyse, to distinguish, to trace change and development rather than uniformity and continuity. Only movement has interest; the static is not significant and anyway is not believed in. Moreover, it is not simply a question of what minds find thinkable; it is also a matter of emotional attraction. For some time now, Christian ecumenism has reckoned with theological pluralism. Sometimes it has been grudgingly accepted as an unavoidable weakness, part of the scene to be recognized, perhaps a stage on the way to eventual unity.

Sometimes it has been welcomed as a sign of intellectual vitality. But still it has generally been regarded as a feature existing within a notional synthesized whole, which is 'there' if not quite observable, a wider unity which one might grasp if one could see a little more clearly. In that case, the emotional investment is still in synthesis and identity.

But for many in the present intellectual climate, the emotional investment is no longer in agreement of this kind. No longer is such harmony even a dream. It has been abandoned not only because it is seen to be unattainable but because it is no longer felt to be particularly desirable. It no longer enters the lists. Instead, diversity and mobility are the signs of strength, the objects of attraction. What can be distinguished from all else – *that* is what is to be observed, evaluated and, if appropriate, admired; of course not in isolation but in its connections with other objects as they help to set off its individuality.

The question is: can Christian theology exist, even flourish, in such an environment of thought, or must it strive to preserve what may increasingly become an enclave of assumptions, at this very fundamental, general and no doubt irrational level, as the only territory within which it can thrive? Does it depend upon some form of the myth of identity, or are models quite different from that represented in the Vincentian Canon not only possible for Christian theology to work with but even perhaps the bases for positive advance? Could they deserve a welcome?

Awareness of the degree to which identity is a myth provides the first step towards acclimatization to the task. But as we pursue it, we should make room for some reassurance of those alarmed! After all, even if through inadequate historical knowledge our fathers did not know how different they were in outlook and teaching from their predecessors, with whom they believed themselves in harmony, our modern discovery of that difference can, from a realistic point of view, hardly upset us very much: however we assess our relationship with our past, we have arrived where we now are without shipwreck! Whether we see the development which has brought us to our present position in terms of identity and essential continuity or in terms of related but diverse responses, within a tradition, to a constantly changing cultural environment; whether we are disposed to emphasize identity of thought with Paul or the dimensions of the gap which separates us from him and unites us rather to our own culture; we are still, if we are worrying the bone of Christian theology at all, placing ourselves within the tradition of faith. To that degree, relativists though we may be, we have let the weight fall on the side of identity and continuity, however far our evaluation of it may differ from that of the past.

But does not even this degree of interest in defining ourselves as our forerunners did betray what may increasingly be felt as an archaic brand of concern with continuity? Is not much of *our* Christianity inevitably an article much more accurately describable as different from that which men held at various periods in the past? Do not its closer affinities lie with the surrounding culture rather than with the tradition by which it sets such store? Am I not linked, whatever I may allege, by far stronger cultural and intellectual ties to my unbelieving neighbour than to my Christian ancestors? Perhaps the very concern with self-definition in relation to the Christian past may show a failure in that analytical integrity which has been described as so prominent a feature of our present culture; perhaps we thus show ourselves as reluctant participators in that culture, or else (for we must not overestimate the degree of its definition) confused actors in the process of its emergence, half tied to old ways, half unsure of the feel of the new.

The conflict may be expressed thus. Integrity demands – it has long been recognized – that we examine, for example, early Christian theology as a phenomenon of its own setting and time, first in itself but then also alongside comparable phenomena of the period. We view it as an element in a total context of first-century religious expression and theological endeavour. We refrain from seeing it as the first stage in the production of the Christianity we know, because we see from many examples that the status of such an approach is dubious and that it is the short road to absurd anachronism in which, for example, later doctrine is too neatly read out of the New Testament and the apostles are painted as amazingly similar to the admired religious leaders of our own day. We see that it is only romantic sentiment, backed by shaky theological principles, the heart and not the head, which leads us to feel so close an affinity with those men. But has that 'sentiment' no reputable backing? Is there not, accessible to human powers of analysis, some reality which over-arches the infinitely complex process of historical causation and which can legitimately link our articulate belief with theirs?

A key may lie in the manner in which and the anxiety with which the connection with the past is asserted. If the theological demand is continually and exclusively for sameness, if the mental look-out is trained to recognize only deviation and then to raise the alarm, disappointment must inevitably ensue, and the defending troops may imagine themselves overwhelmed – by forces whose strength, and aggressive intentions, are in fact illusory. But alter the demand, adopt a different expectation; and peace and freedom may result.

Christian belief is not, on any showing, exhaustively described as holding what the predecessors held. It looks not simply to a tradition of formulation in this world, but chiefly to God. It is in fact within the character of Christian theism that we may find the resources, lying deep as at the bottom of a too often neglected well, from which to evaluate the position afresh. There are within that theism certain instincts, almost intuitive convictions, which belong to a deeper level of belief than fully articulate statement. This is the level from which springs the impulse which makes us theologians now and overarches the gaps of culture which divide us from the past. In terms of what we called 'anxiety' but should describe more positively as the sense of fundamental commitment, perhaps this is the only level which should finally concern us, if we are to retain the capacity to speak significantly in our own culture.

We refer to two of these instincts: first, that God is indescribable; all language about him is inadequate, tentative and provisional. Second, that nevertheless it is possible to relate to him and that a Christian is one who finds that the relating is best done in ways that bear on the figure of Jesus. We take our proposals in turn. They are of course simple and platitudinous. They may be none the worse for that; all will hang on the manner of their treatment.

The first is a commonplace of all thoughtful theism, whether Christian or not. It lies in the roots of the Christian tradition: 'no man has seen God at any time' (John 1.18), a statement grounded in the Old Testament (e.g. Ex. 33.20). But continually this conviction, so clear to every prayerful believer, to everyone who pauses to reflect what 'God' can signify[5], has in practice been suppressed, overwhelmed in the weight of speculative definition and discussion, which, while never denying it, has in practice removed it from consciousness. Yes, God is this, God is that; God is thus, God is not thus. So easily does the detail of definition accumulate, and man who has never seen God at any time comes to feel very familiar with him and in a position to be very voluble about him. But take our ignorance of God seriously and see discourse about him as always having the character of an imaginative endeavour, then faith is freed from taking its formulatory responsibilities too seriously, freed from the duty of eternal adherence to this formula rather than that, able to explore and adapt its standpoint as its sense of the truth at its widest shifts and grows.

Yet there is more. *Christian* faith is not mere free-ranging theism. It has opted, within the theistic possibilities, for that way of responding to God, 'knowing' God, to which Jesus gave decisive shape, whether in himself or in that to which he has given rise. The reasons why a man opts for theism and for this particular kind of theism do not here concern us; at all events, whatever the reasons, here is the point of choice, the point of division between Christian 'belief' and 'unbelief'.

Of course many would feel that to rest content with these two principles as sufficient definition of Christian faith is to be satisfied with something which is far too nebulous – and unnecessarily so, for the resources for ampler statement lie to hand in the Christian store. But our restriction is deliberate. From one point of view it is certainly productive of vagueness. But to go further in the direction of definition is to court inevitably another kind of restriction. It is to adopt a particular idiom, to lean upon a particular style of authority among those open to the Christian, necessarily to the exclusion of others. Yet every one of them is confined in its usefulness by its attachment to a particular intellectual setting or by various inherent disadvantages. Let us examine briefly four examples.

First, the biblical way. If basic Christian faith is given body by means of biblical concepts and themes, it is impossible to avoid the questions raised by their intellectual distance from the present day; impossible also to avoid the charge that an artificial unity is being imposed upon the diverse mass of biblical material, which is the product of innumerable settings, some intentionally at variance with others, and certainly was not assembled with any tightly conceived intellectual coherence in mind.

Second, the way of tradition. If faith is to be amplified from the resources of the Christian tradition, the question of selection poses itself even more urgently, with the attendant risk of arbitrariness and the need to justify the choice of the aspects to which special deference is given. How is it possible to see authority in such a mass of theological material, without using some organizing principle? And how can the choice of such a principle be determined? To place theological trust in 'tradition' is to court either the charge of naivety or else difficulties of method beside which the problems raised by scripture pale into insignificance.

No wonder then that 'tradition' is often interpreted to mean what is in effect a third path of Christian theological activity, the magisterial, that is, finding guidance in the official deliverances of the church, however that may be defined. While winning high marks for deference to accredited authority, this approach can in practice hardly steer clear of inconsistency and risks failure to recognize the pressure of historical circumstance upon the formulation of alleged theological truth. Again, a certain naivety and an anachronistic style of thought follow all too easily.

Fourth, there is what may be called the scholastic way, that is the formation of a structure of Christian theology within the terms of a chosen philosophical scheme. Its virtue is likely to be consistency; its manifest disadvantage is that it commands the assent only of those who can share the particular philosophical basis on which it rests. If that ceases to commend itself, then the theological structure itself ceases to carry conviction.

In practice – and both the historical and the ecclesiastical nature of Christianity press in this direction – Christian theology tends to follow none of these paths exclusively. Few schemes, whatever their champions may avow, stick to one resource, one method. They combine and mix them. To many, this may seem a strength, the using of what has been made available, perhaps by divine providence, perhaps by rich historical development. To others, however, it may seem rather to mean losing the clarity which, whatever the defects, would have followed from pursuing a straighter and narrower way.

We admitted that from one point of view the decision to refrain from adopting one of the four ways of theological procedure just outlined (or, with its attendant obfuscation, a combination of them) was a decision in favour of vagueness. Certainly, elaboration along any of the lines mentioned gives point and definition to belief. But from another point of view, that decision itself produces a kind of sharpness. The basic Christian affirmation, stripped of conceptual clothing, which, however unattractive in itself, restricts movement, now possesses a power derived from its very simplicity; possesses also a potentiality for movement in new directions. The undecked, but unencumbered, faith has the opportunity to thrust forward into new fields. It has the chance to be a gospel for new worlds of thought and cultural enterprise.

The plea for such a restriction of the theological base arose from a recognition of the shifting cultural sands upon which Christian theology has, largely unwittingly, lived out its long and complex existence. The fact of contemporary cultural pluralism leads to precisely the same conclusions and reinforces them. In recognizing both its present intellectual setting and the nature of its past, Christian theology needs to strip itself down, not just for more effective action but also in order that it may be aware of the difference between its basic affirmation and its varied conceptual clothing.

This theological position will then have these characteristics. It will be economical, because circumstances seem to demand the strong statement and exploration of a few things rather than the extensive but inevitably problematic statement of many things. It will be empirical, in the sense of adopting as far as possible the common speech of thoughtful men. The underlying conviction is that the Christian faith is essentially not a complex matter: its apparent complexity derives from the length of its historical existence and the variety of idioms in which it has expressed itself, each leaving a legacy to ensuing generations. It must not be complex if it is to be what it has always alleged; that is, not an esoteric doctrine for the few but a gospel for the many, accessible to those willing to give it their attention. To be released for such accessibility is the urgent present need of theology.

But of course Christian theology cannot confine itself to the mere reiteration of the two basic convictions which we gave as the foundation of all structures which have been and may be built. The Christian at prayer may indeed affirm that nothing else is needful but the contemplation of God as given shape and colour by Jesus. But there will always be the task of turning aside from prayer into speech directed towards other persons, both inside the Christian community and beyond it.

The question then is: by what means, if not one of the four classical methods, can there be extension from the foundation? Is there a way of building which rests squarely upon it yet does not cause the resulting structure to stand forth from the environment as impossibly alien?

There may be a new hope of success if we observe a certain austerity and economy. Let the elaboration of a pattern of belief proceed by asking this question in relation to each area of doctrinal discussion: what, with regard to that area, are the implications of the style of belief in God which is formed by Jesus and that which springs from him? Such a procedure will not only further the aims of economy and simplicity; it will also make for theological coherence and demonstrate the organic character of Christian belief, as everything is seen to spring straight from the foundation. How often the organic character of the faith is obscured as doctrine is considered under discrete headings – trinity, atonement, eucharist, ministry. How often it is obscured even to the extent that developments in a secondary area may effectively belie more fundamental belief, so that Christians find themselves distressed as they see no way to reconcile their underlying conviction of God's saving love with, for example, the ecclesiology or doctrine of ministry which they have come to hold. Further, it is precisely the elaboration of theological structures on the departmental pattern, with insufficient regard for the simple affirmations underlying and supporting them, which has created the weight of culturally alien theology, tenacious but so rapidly dated. A theology which resolutely maintains clear, straight lines from all outlying topics to its basic convictions will have a better chance of adapting itself to changing circumstances, while at the same time escaping self-betrayal.

It is time to bring this sketch of a particular style of theological exploration into relation with the general purpose of this book. Chapters IV and V will show something of its performance in action. Our aim, it will be recalled, is to probe the roots of Christian doctrine in the New Testament and the logic by which those roots began to sprout patterns of belief. To perform this task, we need freedom of manoeuvre. We need too to avoid being restricted by unhelpful or misleading models of the structure and development of belief. We need to approach the phenomena afresh with a kind of direct simplicity which is free from anachronism (i.e. refrains from seeing the early evidence in terms of later doctrinal schemes) and does not ignore the context of thought and culture in which the diverse material of the New Testament has to be evaluated. With the aid of a certain theological frankness, we seek to bring a Christian analysis to bear upon those earliest sources. 'Christian analysis' in the sense that our ultimate aim is to give verbal clothing to the Christian experience of God. Taking this approach, we undertake the programme of soundings outlined at the end of the previous chapter.[6]

III

The Writers

Recent decades have seen a considerable development in the subtlety of perception brought to the study of the thought of the individual New Testament writers. There has been both a greater degree of attention to this aspect of New Testament studies and a greater sharpness of focus than ever before. In certain cases, particularly Paul and John, the movement has not been in principle a novelty: it has been a matter of extending to these writers approaches which were already well established. But in the study of the first three gospels, the change has been nothing less than revolutionary.

As the classification given to them, 'the synoptic gospels', itself indicates, the study of these three documents has centred, during most of the past two centuries, in which critical scholarship has developed, upon the question of the literary relationship between them. Which of the first three gospels is the original? They have much material in common, so which of them used the work of his predecessors, and in what order? Does the material show evidence of sources other than the writings now extant, and how were such sources used? These questions preoccupied scholars in this field almost exclusively over many years. They continue to attract attention, for, despite much work, many hypotheses, and a period when most people thought the matter was settled,[7] the problem remains unsolved. But, as will appear, it can no longer be treated in isolation; indeed, it is partly the introduction of new perspectives which has made it possible to suggest new solutions to the purely literary problem.[8]

An important feature of this preoccupation with the literary question was the diversion of attention from the possibility that the evangelists (apart from John) were constructive or powerful theological thinkers, or even, in any notable way theologically interesting at all. Inevitably, they were treated as organizers of material – arrangers and selectors of sources laid before them. If they were reckoned to have thought theologically, then it was usually only in terms of the simplest and most general ideas concerning Jesus and his preaching.

The other important tool of modern study of the gospels, form criticism, which arose at the time of the First World War, did nothing to remedy this defect.[9] It concentrated on the units of material (stories, groups of sayings, etc.) out of which the gospels seemed to have been formed – on their shape and structure, on their possible development in the tradition of the early Christian congregations by whom they were believed to have been used and transmitted before they reached the writers. Once more, the role of the evangelists was restricted, now to that of editors of units of tradition whose theological content had been largely formed before they reached the point of insertion into the gospels. It is no wonder that the major work of this school, Rudolf Bultmann's *The History of the Synoptic Tradition*,[10] devotes a mere dozen pages to the thought of each of the writers who brought the allegedly so disparate material into literary unity. On this view, it was not at that stage that the theology of the early church made its mark.

But now, since the Second World War, there has been fresh movement. We have had a stream of works which seek to uncover the pattern of each evangelist's thought. Though the work has gone on for a relatively short time, a considerable degree of consensus has emerged. Not surprisingly, this is particularly true of the gospels of Matthew and Luke, where, according to the source-critical orthodoxy with which the writers concerned have generally operated, visible alterations of the Markan basis could be observed as a starting-point for seeking consistent lines of thought in the work of the dependent writer. In the case of Mark, where by comparison the critic is working blind, there has been less agreement, and more in the way of wild shots at the target.[11]

While this line of investigation has flowered most notably in the case of the gospels, where it results from a mode of insight denied to earlier critics, it applies equally well to the more abstract writings, the New Testament epistles, and, as we remarked, has in certain senses long been at work there, particularly in the case of Paul.[12] There emerges then a common approach to the New Testament writings as strongly theological documents, the work of a variety of writers, each with his own distinctive thought and setting in the life of the early church.

The work has been marked by two notable characteristics. By contrast with the widespread assumption until relatively recent days

26

that at least the synoptic gospels spoke, theologically, with something like a single voice, the distinctiveness which marks each of them, along with other writings where its presence has long been more clearly perceived, now stands forth.[13] The validity and status of attempts to present '*the* New Testament view' as a unified piece of teaching becomes more and more problematic. It is apparent that it cannot rest upon any sensitive and close awareness of the patterns of thought represented in the writings, but only, in defiance of such awareness, upon a deliberately distant and generalized view or upon a dogma concerning their unity of outlook which springs from a source outside them and must find its own independent justification.

It has been marked also by a new sensitivity to (combined with greater technical knowledge of) the environment of thought in which these writings were produced. Until relatively recently, even scholarly works presenting an acute analysis of a New Testament writing usually gave the impression that its writer was, in some of the essential lines of his intellectual constitution, a member of the same world as his scholarly critic. Often unconsciously the unifying and bridging power of the Christian tradition, or even just long familiarity, produced this effect, despite longstanding attempts to identify more and more closely the cultural setting in which Christianity arose and in which its first crucial theological developments took place. As a result partly of developments such as a deepening awareness of the techniques of Jewish theologizing and methods of exegesis of texts in the first century, and partly of a shift in perspective which enables the total context of past episodes to be viewed more sharply, the alien quality of the environment in which Jesus taught and in which his followers and opponents reacted to him has become luminous. It serves as a stimulus to constantly renewed alertness in the modern reader or critic as he attempts to enter into the thought of the ancient writer whose work confronts him. It forbids that easy domestication which, while by no means confined to work on the New Testament, perhaps most easily affects those bound by links of faith or ideology to those they read.

But such awareness, while quickening the reader's imagination and saving him from certain kinds of clumsiness and blindness, cannot solve all his problems. It may serve to confront him with a further battery of questions. Beyond the most elementary work of verbal translation, what value can any attempt at interpretation possess? What exactly has been accomplished when the modern exegete produces his account of what Paul or John was saying? He has attempted, using all available technical aids and deliberately bringing his imagination to the task, to enter Paul's mind and re-think his thoughts, follow the movement of his mind. But the more aware he is of the demands of his chosen task, the more conscious he is that in the very attempt at identification he retains his detachment. The more serious the former, the clearer the latter appears. The very work of interpretation recedes like a mirage. What sought to be objective seems more and more to be acutely subjective.

There is no escape from this frustrating paradox in the work of interpretation and exposition. But like many apparent enemies it may, when looked at with fresh eyes, turn out to be a friend. Our own interests, education and culture determine what, for us, Paul 'meant'. If he heard our account of it, he would no doubt deny its truth – and repeat what he first said! But the failure of our attempt to reach Paul's meaning may at any rate reinforce our conviction (cf. p. 16) that uniformity and identity of belief are a chimera never to be found and that the quest for them can only frustrate and deaden vitality of mind. Freshness of theological statement will flourish all the more for not hankering after illusory fidelity to the thought of venerable writers, and interpretation falls into its proper place once it can accept itself as speaking, however scientific its methods, the interpreter's mind.

In what follows, it is inappropriate and unnecessary, in view of scholarly work to which we have referred, that we should do more than paint in broad strokes the outlines of the theological patterns represented by some of the leading New Testament writers. But as we proceed, we shall recognize the factors which we have just described. In attempting to set them in their own context of thought, we disclose our own. The more sharply we perceive them, the more our view is revealed as one among any number of possibilities. But at least we shall seek to free them from one kind of distorting apparatus commonly attached to them: the assumption that as Christian belief now is, so it ever was. In that respect, we shall try to let them provide the agenda; for our aim is to explore the patterns and colours of Christian doctrine as it first stirred into life. Only then shall we be able to assess their effect upon us, and decide what leaves we may take from their book and, having taken them, how we may use them to reclothe in words our own experience of God.

PAUL

The theology of Paul may be described as monotheism in which God

28

was pre-eminently open to relationship with man – if the way could only be found. The chief and only important religious task was to discover the path of access and then to take it. It was a theology at the heart of which, within the scope of the quest, was a crisis and a transformation. The occasion of the crisis was Jesus: but we had better say 'Jesus', because Paul's reflection upon him so obscured the means by which the historical Jesus himself brought about the crisis that we can only guess what they were. To him, they may well have seemed direct, vivid, and clearer than anything else in his experience. To us, seeking historians' answers to historians' questions, they seem indirect and obscure. At that level, Paul tells us little.

The crisis was within the context of the quest for access to God, a quest which Paul's Judaism already provided him with the means to undertake. First and foremost, the law, as elaborated in scribal tradition, offered the chance of life pleasing to God and so of acceptance by him. The law was the summation of God's revelation. Though that revelation had taken place in history, in Paul's eyes it was to be found less in awareness of a long and eventful past than in knowledge of a book – the writings of the Old Testament. For him, Abraham was a crucial figure in a theological literature, much more than a character of the distant past. But that literature itself had taken on new shape and fresh proportions by virtue of the crisis. For now 'Jesus' occupied the place and role formerly taken by the law and was the means of being accepted by God.

Now a historical figure can only perform such a task if he becomes symbolic – is given to wear a *persona* which the bare chronicler of his life would find no words to notice. So in Paul, Jesus has become the bearer of elaborate symbolism, centering however, upon a sequence of events in which he was the actor: death, burial, and resurrection. There is no reason to suppose that Paul, unlike us who face 'miracle' as a question, felt any reason to pause before mentioning the last of those events in the same breath as the others. For him, they formed a single complex. Together, they made the act by which God had opened valid access to himself for those able to receive it. Or rather they formed the climax of it: the act had begun with the descent of Jesus from the heavenly realm into the world (Phil. 2.6ff.). Thus his capacity to perform the act was comprehensively assured – from his remotest source (he was pre-existent) to his final goal, he was accredited by God.

But theological attention centred on his death and resurrection. The transformation Paul knew as a result of Jesus was of such a character that in his view it could be accounted for by exploring the significance of Jesus in relation to that dual episode. This realization is itself explained by the nature of the hindrances to man's access to God and the nature of the action required to remove them. The first and perhaps the most far-reaching of the hindering forces was the personal spiritual powers which were so prominent in the cosmological picture most widespread in the world of Paul's day. These powers were seen as responsible for what would now be called the non-moral evils which beset human life, such as disease and natural catastrophe, but because the powers were personal even these evils took on moral status: they were acts of malevolence launched against man by rebellious subordinates of God, the ruler of the universe. The removal of their power must be brought about by their defeat and extinction, or by their absorption and reconciliation with the power of God. Briefly and without elaboration, Paul expressed his new sense of the powerlessness of these evils to hinder access to God and his awareness of God's graciousness, by holding that Jesus had accomplished both these objects. In Col. 2.14f. and I Cor. 2.8, also implicitly Rom.8.35–9, we read of the removal of these powers by their defeat; in Col. 1.15–20, by their reconciliation to the one creator God.

The second and much more ambiguous hindering force was the law itself. Ambiguous, because while it was a gift of God and in principle a means to serve him and so obtain access to him, it now seemed, from Paul's transformed standpoint, to be in practice, and even by its very nature, a gift that was at best limited and temporary, at worst harmful and obstructive. Paul gave mythological – as it seems to us – expression to this ambiguity by saying that the law came not directly from God's hand but by the mediation of angels (Gal. 3.19). It came from him – yes, but at one remove. In so far as it was temporary, the law had been succeeded by a more perfect way of access to God – that resulting from his surrounding grace (Gal. 3.24) and described on the human side as 'faith', an unconditioned willingness to receive God's graciousness and to take the path of access now opened. In so far as it was harmful and obstructive, the law had been transcended by the more perfect regime in which God's grace and man's faith met each other and made possible the new style of relationship between the two. In relation to the law, it was not possible to think in terms of mere defeat or removal or even reconciliation: its ambiguity demanded more subtle treatment, some kind of meeting of its legitimate requirements. To meet this demand, felt so strongly in the very core of his Pharisee's moral and intellectual awareness, Paul interpreted Jesus' act in terms of a transaction without which the observable and felt result could never have been reached. The law's requirement of man's perfect response to its terms, its demand for 'righteousness', had been met in principle by Jesus, not only in his 'knowing no sin' (II Cor. 5.21) but even as, by enduring crucifixion, he underwent the law's curse (Gal. 3.13). By thus submitting to the law's terms, Jesus had most satisfyingly, according to the almost aesthetic requirements of Paul's mental patterns, opened the way to that access to God of whose availability he was supremely convinced.

The third hostile force lay more clearly within man himself. 'More clearly' certainly, yet not wholly so. For Paul, even sin, which might seem to be the place where human responsibility enters into its own, could appear as an external force invading man and causing him to fall. The story of the fall of Adam and Eve in Genesis 3 lay to hand to encourage such a picture, and the belief in evil powers found yet another expression in this more intimate sphere (cf. Rom. 7.8,11). But if that were all, then Paul would present us with a picture of man's ills in which his responsibility played no part. Both his predicament (including his moral failure and perversity) and his rescue would be the work of wholly outside forces. That man can only with extreme injustice be held fully responsible for his state is an element in Paul's analysis which raises the greatest sympathy in modern readers, however differently they would formulate it. But to take his share of responsibility, to be answerable for himself, is essential to his humanity. So sin or 'the flesh' (his characteristic term for this earth-bound and self-centred dimension of man's life, both mental and physical) are also present in the heart of man's consciousness; and it is here that the most radical reversal, the core of the crisis, takes place. It arises not from within man himself or even (Paul felt no pressure to safeguard this) with man's consent, but by the impulse of divine power establishing a quite new principle of existence, a wholly fresh sphere for life: the term for it was 'spirit' – a word which nicely ranged in sense from signifying God's mode of being and activity to the principle in man which could rise up to meet the irruption of God's power (I Cor. 2. 10–16).

In this sphere too Paul knew the transforming effect of Jesus. He could express it only by what reads like a rather confused identification of the activity of Jesus with the power of God (cf. the use of 'spirit' language in Rom. 8). He was aware of a wholly new principle of direction, of which Jesus was the source and content (Gal. 2.19f.).

He had carried out a task whose effect had been to bring about that state of affairs in man's relationship with God which in Paul's view had always been the object of human existence. No wonder then that in seeking to expound the significance of Jesus he was driven to set him in parallel with Adam – for Jesus had both set up and exemplified the reality given to Adam but then so disastrously thrown away (Rom. 5.12ff.; I Cor. 15.22). No wonder that he could acclaim him as Messiah (*christos*) – for clearly he had carried out God's purposes of salvation for his people, but at a level both more comprehensive and more profound than that of contemporary Jewish hope. No wonder that he found most fitting of all the description of Jesus as God's 'Son' (Rom. 8.32; Gal. 1.16) – for this most plainly 'hit off' the all-embracing nature of his achievement in representing God to man and consummating his age-old purpose.

It was the 'Adam' level in Paul's conception of Jesus' significance which led to his sense of both its universality and its corporateness, or rather was the key to its intellectual expression. If Jesus' action seemed to Paul to demand interpretation at that fundamental human level, then it must be valid in principle for all men. This was far from being an exercise in humanistic theory: it sprang by a kind of theological elegance from his underlying belief in God as creator, now given renewed life by his Christian experience. Because his pattern of thought (formed by his Jewish training) expressed itself naturally by means of symbolic, inclusive figures, Paul found it natural to see those who had received the new dispensation of 'grace', 'faith' and 'spirit' as bound together – they were all 'in Christ'. Sometimes, when the 'Adam' pattern was in mind, they were seen as a kind of new start to the human race (II Cor. 5.17). Sometimes, they could be described as a new Israel (Gal. 6.16), that is, when the historical perspective of God's promises to his people was to the fore (Rom. 9–11). It depended on circumstance, and there was no inevitable logic linking the different strands in his thought; they arose naturally from different strands in his experience. But the conviction of life 'in Christ' came at the end of them all and united them. It was life brought into being as a result of God's Messiah who was the source of new hope for any who entered into fellowship with their Creator's Son.

The tone and setting of Paul's thought was eschatological; that is, it was tied to a sense that the end of the world, or, more precisely, God's decisive intervention in its affairs for judgment and salvation, was very near. Indeed, so intense was his own experience of transformation in his relationship with God as a result of Jesus, that he could not but express it in the only appropriate theological vocabulary available to him – that of the Jewish eschatological expectation. It was from this source that he was able to speak of the new awareness as the activity of God's 'spirit' (Rom. 8. 1ff.; I Cor. 12.13); to see it as a judgment already made and God's righteousness already revealed (cf. Rom. 1–4); to describe existence in the light of the new awareness as 'risen' life (Rom. 6.1–11; Col. 3.1) and linked to resurrection in Jesus (I Cor. 15.21ff.), for the resurrection of the dead, like the outpouring of the Spirit, was part of the promise for the new age. All these were different ways of describing the one experience, highlighting different aspects of it. The symptoms of that age were now everywhere discernible; or, we might say, Paul was able without strain to interpret his new found experience of God, resulting from Jesus, in categories drawn from the wonderful hope for God's coming act upon which he had been reared.

Paul's theology may be described as a monotheism which had been not so much altered as revitalized as a result of Jesus. Some of its most important outlines had received quite new definition above all, it was now clear that God was gracious and that his will to give man acceptance and access was wholly reliable. To account for the new consciousness to which he had come, Paul told the simple theological story of Jesus' coming, death and resurrection. He seems to have put no emphasis, at least for his central purposes, on his teaching or incidents of his career. His death and resurrection above all, seen as a drama in which God was in action, dealing decisively with forces which had ruined man's relationship with him, had been the crisis leading to the transformation which was the centre of Paul's theological awareness.

THE PASTOR, FOLLOWER OF PAUL

Within the New Testament we have the work of two writers who issued their productions, pseudonymously, under the name of Paul. In the case of the first, the writer of Ephesians, it is evident, from the saturation of his work with Pauline words and phrases, that he saw himself as enunciating pure paulinism. Indeed, despite our present assumption, it is not every critic who is prepared to deny that he is distinguishable enough from Paul to be other than the master himself. But in the case of the writer of I Timothy, II Timothy and Titus, there is general admission that the case is more problematic. It is quite impossible to decide whether this writer, who occupies us in this section, saw himself as conveying authentic Pauline thought as it applied to the circumstances which confronted him or as putting forth his own ideas, adopting only Paul's name. But in favour of the former hypothesis is the fact that despite many religious interests and linguistic features quite different from Paul's, there are more resemblances than appear at first sight to Paul's undoubted writings, especially Romans. It is probable that the writer had every intention of speaking with his master's voice in circumstances which, he believed, desperately needed his authoritative guidance.

This is not the place to go in detail into these off-key reminiscences of Paul's writings.[14] Nor is it the place to consider whether this writer's work may illustrate the difficulties of *bona fides* interpretation (assuming that he really did set out to give genuine Pauline teaching), and how far a man may read even in a near predecessor only what his eyes make it easy for him to see. We must examine the shape of this writer's theology in its own right, and must not be surprised to find that it is notably different from Paul's and in some respects remarkably so. But first, we offer one caution. So far, we have been speaking of 'the writer' and 'the writing' as if they were simple alternatives. Of course we cannot be sure, especially when we have only brief examples of a writer's work, that we have a balanced picture of his thought. In the case of Paul, we have enough, and he must take his chance. The same may go for the evangelists. But the case of the Pastor is less clear. Is it fair to judge him on such short writings, to take it that he did not think what he did not write within this brief compass? We may be encouraged in thinking it not unfair to do so, by the fact that he includes within these works a number of succinct statements of belief which look as if they were meant to be definitive and authoritative – and so, we may assume, to all intents and purposes, exhaustive, as far as his central belief was concerned.

What then was that belief? He was a monotheist: 'there is one God' (I Tim. 2.5). He did not live in an environment sufficiently sophisticated intellectually or so exclusively Christian and Jewish for him to take it for granted; it was worth stating. His conception of monotheism was in line with that of the more thoughtful Greek and Jewish religion of his day – the one God was in himself inaccessible, unless there were a means of mediation. For this writer, there was precisely that: alone of the New Testament writers he gives to Jesus this title. 'There is one mediator between God and men'. '*One* mediator' – as distinct from a number of them. For him, as for Paul, Jesus had superseded existing bearers of that role. In this case, it seems that Moses was the one upon whom he saw Jesus to be

34

modelled. Just as Moses had repeatedly stood before the people on God's behalf and before God as their supplicant (cf. e.g. Ex. 32), so now had Jesus. The stories of Israel's wanderings in the wilderness after the exodus were the source of his conception. This mediator – the one 'in the middle' – was distinctly from the human side: he was 'the man Christ Jesus, who gave himself as a ransom for all' (2.6). But (following a probable translation of Titus 2.13), he was also from the divine side – 'our God', or, perhaps, 'our deity', as distinct from other people's deities.

If that was who Jesus was, his achievment was expressed mainly in other terms. Again, they owed something to current language about Moses, but there was also a debt to the cult of emperors. Jesus had *manifested himself* – and would do so again (II Tim. 4.1); and he had done it in order to be a *saviour*. These two ideas, related to each other in the religious setting which had formed the writer, dominated his mind when he sought to express, generally in brief but powerful formulas, the heart of his belief: see especially II Tim. 1.9f.; Titus 3.4ff. As 'saviour', Jesus was in line with God, who, as in the Old Testament, could also bear this title. He might have a mediator to act for him, but still salvation was his own characteristic work (Titus 2.10). Both these terms are, in the main, distinctive of this writer within the New Testament.

The most succinct and comprehensive statement of faith which he gives is at first sight uncharacteristic of him, and we are made to wonder whether he had not simply taken it over without necessarily finding it wholly congenial to his mind. Its tone is more speculative than anything else in these writings. In I Tim. 3.16 there is a hymn-like formula which describes the work and achievement of Jesus in heaven and on earth.[15] Here most notably (but in fact in these writings as a whole) we are confronted by a feature to which we must accustom ourselves: it is not what this formula affirms, but what it omits which is striking. Or rather (for why should we assume a norm with which there should be compliance?), we notice the quite distinctive form of this pattern of belief. Neither here nor anywhere in these writings is there any explicit reference to the theological significance of the death or resurrection of Jesus as such. We say 'as such' because if we were to start from the assumption that 'they must be there somewhere', then indeed we could find them, apparently somewhat loosely described, even obscured or glossed over. Certainly Jesus 'gave himself' (I Tim. 2.6; Titus 2.14); but whether this expression is a reference to his death or to his 'coming into the world', which, according to I Tim. 1.15, is what he did 'in order to save sinners', is left open. Certainly he who manifested himself was 'received up in glory' (I Tim. 3.16), but by what means and as a result of what event is left without mention. Certainly he 'set death at nought' (II Tim. 1.10), but whether by some dramatic exposition of his own death, or at his exaltation to heaven, or by what means, we cannot tell. The reference to Jesus 'risen from the dead' in II Tim. 2.8 is totally without elaboration.

On the evidence of his words, this writer leaves the impression that for him Jesus was the one who came and 'appeared' at the cost of himself, who by his 'appearing' effected rescue from sin and mortality, and who will once more 'appear' in judgment. That is his favoured doctrinal idiom. Impelled no doubt by the needs of his times and circumstances, this writer is more concerned with the stability in orthodox belief and morals which, in an ordered community of faith, followed on from this work of Jesus, than with the exploration of the meaning of the work itself. For doctrinal purposes, he repeats the language of his faith but he does not reach out for words which will express it vividly or profoundly. In that respect, he is, theologically, a lesser man than Paul. Even if he tried to repeat words and phrases which he learnt from Paul, his cast of mind was quite different. For him, that which was central for Paul was without doctrinal interest. Jesus' death and resurrection, the core of divine action and the point of crisis in Paul's view, where his theological imagination found its well-spring, received no more than bare reference. 'Saving manifestation' was for him the core of Jesus' purpose and accomplishment. This was the language in which he found it natural to clothe his conviction that as a result of Jesus a new light had dawned, a new hope had been given, and man's need had been met. He does not explain why it should have been so, sufficient for him that Jesus was the one accredited and wholly sufficient for the task.

MARK

At the beginning of this chapter, we showed why and how the gospels have only recently been appreciated as writings of 'high theology content'. We referred also to the fact that it had been proved peculiarly difficult to identify that content in the case of Mark, partly because this gospel is generally believed both to have been written before Matthew and Luke and to have been used by them, so that it cannot be compared with predecessors to discover patterns of thought in alterations made; partly because it seems to have, for modern readers at least, an inherently elusive quality.

There is some reason to think that this is more than a matter of cultural distance between Mark and ourselves, and that the writer of this gospel set high store by mysteriousness in the understanding and statement of religious truth.

Nevertheless, while some attempts to crack Mark's secret account for so little of him as to be bizarre and while a number of scholars still refuse to believe that his thought was particularly subtle, something like a consensus begins to emerge on the general outline of his ideas.

For Mark, God's purposes were at the same time deeply mysterious (4.10–12; 8.11; and sayings like those in 15.34 or 14.22–5) and vividly decisive in the fulfilment they had now received (1.14f.). This fulfilment centred on Jesus and in him their ambiguous and mysterious character had its sharpest focus. On the one hand, what he had done and taught (Mark draws no clear line between the two – for him, to act as Jesus acted was 'teaching', cf. 1.21f., then 1.27, as a response to an act of healing) was 'gospel' – a message-bringing-salvation, itself a kind of fusion of word and deed (1.1), certainly a message leading not just to knowledge but to a transformed state of affairs. But this message is not, in Mark, bound up noticeably with carefree joy. Though it is linked with release from ills and burdens, as the miracle stories, included as pictures of Jesus' deeper meaning, show, yet it is more closely associated with suffering and death (8.31–9.1; 10.35–45). The nexus between 'gospel' and 'death' is the point at which Mark worries from start to finish. He knows it to be the key to true understanding and so to life, yet there seems to be a sense in which the deep enigma of it baffled him. Much of his thought is bound up with his attempt to tease out this mystery, especially when he seems to be controverting other ways of interpreting Jesus which take too little account of it. This lies behind the prominence given to the episode of Peter's inadequate and mistaken confession (8.27ff.) and that of the disciples' quest for greatness (10.35ff.). It seems to lie behind the special (but never openly explained) significance given to the title 'Son of Man'. Whatever it meant in Jesus' own circle, for Mark it was the way to correct the understanding of Jesus as Messiah – a title of pure triumph – by saying that suffering was of the essence of his task (10.45), even if triumph would follow. The glory would be that of the Son of Man, that is, the one who suffered (14.62).

Mark did not resolve the tension between 'gospel' and 'suffering', but he was clear that it was divinely authorized (1.1–11; 9.2ff.) – despite the cry from the cross (15.34). He also believed that this truth was very difficult to receive, even for those who are called to Jesus' service and friendship (1.16–20; then 6.52; 8.14–21). Perhaps he meant by these latter passages, obscure as they are, that eucharistic fellowship, cast by Mark into the heart of the passion story (14.22–5), will in the end enable a follower to perceive; though the two-sidedness persists, cf. 14.28 and 16.7, with 14.50.

If 'Son of Man' helps to communicate the essential understanding of Jesus as the one who must suffer, 'Son of God' asserts the divine authorization of his whole work: 1.11; 9.7. It is understood by the evil powers (3.11) and its acceptance is the foundation of faith (15.39). That authorization is the basis of Mark's own faith as he contemplates and tries to expound what Jesus can then signify. In his suffering and then in that of his followers (8.35; 10.38) Mark believes he has found the vein he must follow. And everything else is subordinate to that, even Jesus' triumph – assured though that is. That too is bound up with suffering. It emerged mysteriously from his death (16.1–8) and its astonishing final disclosure to his followers will come out of persecution and hardly imaginable catastrophes (13).

In the proportions of Mark's theology, suffering and death loom very large. According to him, you could only see the truth of God if you kept your eyes relentlessly upon them. In the end, Mark's is a contemplative theology, not lending itself to full statement in words and neat ideas. But he is sure of the path along which God is to be found; sure that it comes from Jesus; sure too that God gave it in giving him.

MATTHEW

Assuming that Mark wrote his gospel first, then it is evident that Matthew used the greater part of his work. But he added to it and altered it, with the result that, as we shall see, he depicts the mission of Jesus in quite different colours.

In comparison with Mark, Matthew produces a picture characterized by comprehensiveness and clarity. He is not concerned that we should contemplate a simple but profound mystery; he is interested in our 'getting it right', both in theological understanding and in conduct of life. For him, God has made himself quite plain over all essential areas, and only the perverse (the Jews) can possibly mistake him. Hence the virulence of chapter 23 and the condemnation of all who refuse Jesus and his message (10.14f.; 13.11ff.; 21.33–46). God has made himself plain by prophetic declaration and visible temporal process (the genealogy of Jesus, tracing his ancestry back to Abraham, announces it from the start, 1.1–17). In Matthew more than any other New Testament writer – though all shared the essence of his belief in the matter – prophecy led to fulfilment as day leads to night, and to point to it was to bring argument to an end. For this reason, Matthew's underlying view of God's manner of working leaves most modern readers asking questions: he does not go deep enough. His interest centres on two other aspects of Jesus as the one sent by God: he is the bestower of a comprehensive way of life and he is the founder of the church. While Matthew often 'tinkers' with Mark's work as he received it, in order to express secondary features of his outlook (such as his admiration for the disciples as models of obedient understanding or his dislike of attributing to Jesus crude techniques to produce miraculous healings[16]), he boldly adds to it long passages of teaching by Jesus designed to provide guidance for all the main eventualities of Christian life as he knew it: the bases of moral and religious duty (5–7), the conditions and expectations of Christian witness (10), the broad characteristics of the church's life and growth (13), the proper spirit and methods of the church's discipline and cohesion (18) and the nature of the world's end and how to face it (24–5).

It is a picture coloured by the life of an institution (the church) within a providential time-scheme, reaching back to Abraham (1.2) and on to the judgment (25.31–46), but dominated and decisively redirected and interpreted by Jesus. Redirected not in the sense of diverted from its proper path, but in the sense of set forth anew upon its way. With his deep attachment to the law (5.17–20; 23.3,23) and to God's chosen community (though, oddly, he never makes much of the church as a 'new Israel'), he refuses to allow us to press him into deciding whether Judaism was regrettable or merely perverse and faithless, a mistake or just mistaken.

Yet while he retains these powerful orientations from Judaism (law and chosen community), Jesus is decisive for him – as the intended one, the Messiah, the one who goes the way he must go (3.15). His death seems to be seen along these lines – for the passion story itself Matthew is significantly content to take over Mark, embellishing his account with a few additions, none of them theologically central, most of them simply heightening Jewish responsibility (for aiding the fulfilment of God's plan?!) or helping on the growth of legend.[17]

Taking it strictly as theology, that is as the expression of ideas about God, there is then a certain simplicity about the work of Matthew. Questions are asked and answered at the level at which for him they were raised, and with that level he rests content. This is as true of his account of the place of Jesus as it is of his underlying belief in God. God oversees all things and brings about the fulfilment of his purposes for all men (28.19) through the teaching, death and triumph of Jesus, his chosen one. If we ask why these things should be, Matthew's only answer is that God intended it so and announced it beforehand in sources anyone might see and (perhaps with scribal help, 13.52) understand. Beyond that, he will not take us, and he saw no need to enquire.

LUKE

One mode of discourse excludes another, or at any rate imposes certain limitations upon its versatility. We distinguish between a fairy story and a text-book on mathematics, and even though it would be possible, in order to sugar the pill, to present the latter in the guise of the former, the attempt would founder before very long and the fairy-tale mask would fall from the face. Much more so than Matthew before him, though in continuity with him, the author of the third gospel and Acts acted as one who believed that theology and story-telling can be a single operation.

In this respect, he is as far as possible from Paul, who showed practically no story-telling propensities at all and may well have been 'tone deaf' to the theological potentiality of stories. The indications are that this belief was not one that he worked up, he just assumed it. As one familiar with the Old Testament, the live literary traditions of Judaism, and those of the Hellenistic world with which they were intertwined, he was simply continuing a tradition which had formed him.

But the choice of the mode (even if calling it a choice is rating it at too high a level of consciousness) limits the operation. There are certain theological concepts which can only imperfectly be expressed in narrative, even if it is generously interlarded with speeches, which give an opportunity, it might seem, to be more abstract and so to have something like the best of both worlds; other concepts whose subtlety simply cannot be conveyed in that mode at all. And adopting a narrative framework imposes implicitly certain ideas which may be difficult to handle outside this mode. To tell a story – the dominant concern – in which God and his agents are central actors is to invite a crudity of belief about the structure of God's dealings with the world conveniently describable as 'the upstairs-downstairs model'. The Greek myths are its most familiar flowering. Luke–Acts is a much less thoroughgoing example: it came from a tradition which contained a number of restraints. Judaism tempered anthropomorphism with the conviction of God's wonderful 'otherness'.

Still, narrative, the orderly and intelligible flow of events, is the method (Luke 1.1–4), and it is executed vividly and attractively throughout. It is done so well that its awkward junctions and loose ends pass most readers by. It takes a specialist to spot them and they are not our present concern.

For our question is: what theology is implicit in this work? Does the narrative mode preclude the expression of profound ideas? At all events, what are the outlines of the picture of God and his activity to which this writer gave expression in his long work?

As with Matthew, the concept is time-centred – and the sweep is even wider: the genealogy of Jesus is carried right back to 'Adam, son of God' himself (Luke 3.38). Again like Matthew, Luke gives shape to time by means of the recurring process of prophecy and fulfilment; but he treats it in a manner altogether less wooden and more flexible and thoroughgoing. With him, it is woven right into the texture of the story, instead of being stamped on to its surface like a series of labels on a package indicating the nature of its contents. Thus the general principle is given in passages like Luke 24.27, 44 and 16.31. But it is worked out beautifully in the stories of annunciation and birth in chapters 1 and 2, where the actions and words of the characters are a recapitulation of Luke's view of the ideal of Old Testament piety: the best in the old is the very womb of the new. It is worked out also when Jesus is portrayed as like the wonderfully bestowed offspring of the Old Testament, such as Samuel (compare the birth stories about Jesus with those about Gideon in Judges 6, Samson in Judges 13 and Samuel in I Sam. 1–2); or as like Moses, as when his teaching takes up and improves upon Moses' law (compare, for example, the invalid reasons for refusing the invitation in Luke 14.18 with the similar reasons, then valid, for escaping military service listed in Deut. 20.5–8; 24.5); or as like Elijah (compare Luke 7.11–17 with the story in I Kings 17, and contrast Luke 9.54f. with II Kings 1.10ff.). And the principle of fulfilment spreads out into the story of the early church, as the acts of the disciples mirror those of Jesus (cf. the reflection of Jesus' trials and death in the treatment accorded to Stephen in Acts 6–7, Peter in Acts 12, and Paul in Acts 21ff.[18]; and the reproducing of Jesus' healings in the work of his apostles, e.g. compare Acts 9.32ff. with passages like Luke 8.40ff.). Intended as no mere literary device, this web of allusions gives shape to the flow of history and shows it to be overruled by God.

But having decided to tell a story of events in this world (however providential) – the life of the chosen man, Jesus, then the activities of his followers – Luke has to take the consequences and his work must suffer inevitable limitations. Thus, at the level of earthly story, the death which concludes the life of an admirable or heroic man can only be a tragedy, and the better the story is told the more poignant must be the end. So it is with Luke's Jesus: his passion story draws more tears than all the rest, because the story predominates and theological interpretation is not interposed (cf. the pathos of the supper scene (Luke 22.14–38), most of it Luke's alone, and the encounters with the women in 23.27–31 and with the penitent, admiring thief in 23.42f.). If there is triumph here, it is the humanistic triumph of heroic virtue. Given Luke's model, God's triumph can only be by the intellectually crude action of a solidly terrestrial resurrection – Luke's risen Jesus is more 'solid' than that of any of the other gospels, though even he cannot be recognized easily (cf., e.g. 24.42f.; 24.16 then 24.31,35). Such a resurrection, springing straight from Luke's strictly narrative method, leaves all the theoretical questions unanswered (what does such a bodily resurrection *mean*?) and responds to one kind of devotional aspiration. So the Emmaus story invites 'religious' translation: yes, we *do* know Jesus when we meet to break the bread, and our knowing him *is* 'unveiled' in that act. But if the story means that, is it also history?

Similarly, with the church. The narrative mode, the decision to tell the tale of how the gospel spread, raises the necessity of a terminus. In the setting of Luke's time, the 'Jerusalem to Rome' scheme is admirable: we move from the holy centre (abandoned by Luke's day in its religio–political role and perhaps discarded by many Christians for any sacred significance) to the imperial centre. The symbolism, with its augury for the future mission, is striking. But its theological significance for later times is faulty. The theological (so called) symbolism only works in the circumstances of Luke's day or while Rome is in some sense the centre of the world. As every half-believing schoolteacher knows, once that is past, Acts becomes mere story; theology does not obtrude.

Sometimes the story suffers for attempting to be the bearer of theological truth. Luke tells the story of the church's early days and no doubt idealizes: as far as its internal life goes, almost all is sweetness and light under the Holy Spirit's lead. Yet a developing institution grows by making decisions, facing questions, and erecting a structure of authority. So the church had to decide on what terms Gentiles might join Jews within its membership. Paul could argue straight from his view of Christ to flat equality in the matter (cf., p. 32).

Luke, characteristically, took a more temporally sensitive view and one shaped by his feeling for the fulfilment of promises cast forth long ago. So, in Acts 15, we learn how the leaders of the church, in solemn council, agreed to admit Gentiles (God having, by miracle, already signified that it must be so and *was* so in Acts 10–11 – a nice mixing of the 'upstairs' and 'downstairs' levels of Christian decision-making). But it was done on condition of such obedience to the Jewish Law as would signify to ears attuned the fulfilment of the day of triumphant entry into the land of promise.[19] But we search in vain (almost) for evidence that these rules were ever widely applied: they seem to be best explained as the result of Luke's being determined by the pattern of his story and his leading principles for understanding the action of God. It shows how powerful they were.

Theologically, his picture was from the Old Testament. In a sense, he never outgrew, theologically, the piety he portrayed so lovingly in his first two chapters. He was a monotheist whose God moved exclusively in the historical dimension. God's intentions were simple and wonderfully beneficent. Like the Pastor, Luke liked the word 'salvation' (Luke 19.9) and the sense of total well-being under God which it signified. Certainly it would be consummated in a future order of whose advent Jesus was the undoubted harbinger (Luke 21). But in the meantime, there was life in the church, impelled by the Spirit and with the stirring example of Jesus' life and death together with his present lordship constantly before the eyes. Even so, anxious forebodings about church life were beginning: Acts 20.29ff. is the saddest thing he wrote, with its sense of developments for which his simple view of smoothly providential church-history-within-world-history was theologically inadequate. The God-given progress was in danger of being halted, its achievements fragmented.

A Christian view of history relying too heavily on the story of the early church, and hence, inevitably, on the presentation in Luke–Acts, has never been able to think very subtly (as distinct from edifyingly) about the church's relationship with society at large or 'the meaning of history'. If we look at these writings within their context and on their own terms, we shall not find that surprising. The approach gave scope for vividness, but precluded profundity. Still, we may be grateful that this writer embraced history and society as he expressed his faith, and did not turn his face from them.

Theologically, Luke asked the questions which story-telling as he understood it imposed upon him. They led him to take a certain view of the providential supervision of human affairs and special divine action which came to a head, wonderfully, in Jesus. For the rest, his interests were in morality and 'the quality of life'. Here, Jesus was the model. Life under God must be lived in imitation of Jesus now in heaven, inspiring us, through the Spirit, sent as a kind of gracious substitute for his own intimate presence, which was now to be best encountered in the pages of this writing. It is the programme for simple (and for most purposes sufficient) Christianity. In a sense, it raises permanent outcry against the theologically minded who persist in wanting more. Paul, for example, might complain of a failure of rationale, especially about Jesus' death and resurrection.

JOHN

John is the reverse of Luke. For him, narrative is the servant of conceptual theology, not its master. So despite his narrative framework his work centres on a small group of compactly linked ideas, expressed in a narrow vocabulary. The book is recognizably of the same genre as the other gospels, but it is the tightest piece of theology in the early church, less fecund but more orderly than Paul. It may owe him some debts, but if so it has developed beyond him and reached relatively settled shape. That does not mean that it left no questions to be asked or that there was delay in asking them. Theology, even Johannine theology within the varied theologizing of the early congregations, did not stand still.

It is customary to say that the Fourth Gospel has the most advanced christology in the New Testament: only here is Jesus undoubtedly called divine (1.1; 20.28). It would be as true (and perhaps more fitting to the perspective of the times) to say it contained the most ample theism.

There was one God, of course; but his relationship with the world consisted of enveloping it with divinity, in close embrace. The 'upstairs-downstairs' model of simple pictorial faith could not do justice to the intense awareness of living in a 'divine environment' (Teilhard de Chardin was a very Johannine Christian). The opening verses of the gospel make this awareness evident. Whatever the tensions and qualifications, the gospel rests upon cosmology and belief in God as creator. In one sense, Jesus is no more than (what more could one want?) his self-expression.

That conviction rests upon Jewish foundations, deeply dug. Experience and the current religious sensibility made serious inroads upon it; and as part and parcel of his general profundity, John was more acutely affected by them than perhaps any other major New Testament writer. (His lesser follower, who wrote the first Johannine epistle, even more so: 2.15ff.; 5.19.) Confidence in the world as truly expressing God the creator faltered. Evil was a great lord, whose

44

power of darkness encroached and threatened extremely, so that the circle of light was a precious and blessed haven where those admitted could rest content.[20] There, God could be known and experienced.

The existence of the haven, which was in effect the Christian community, was due to Jesus (17.16–19). How John would have reconciled it with his more visionary sense of Jesus' universal scope (12.32), we cannot tell: at this point, we may suppose that practical experience of small-scale, intensely valued church life dictated the balance of theological pattern. But the account of Jesus was certainly of the widest dimensions. He was the Word – the comprehensive agent of enveloping divinity. Enveloping not just spatially but also temporally: in this perspective, he who had done so much must not be merely deserving of the highest titles during his life-time and of divine honours after his time in the world, but also pre-existent, eternal in every direction (1.1; 8.58). So because (as we might say) Jesus had made such a comprehensive difference, he received from John the most comprehensive acclaim. In him, strands from many areas of Jewish theology about God's self-communication to man and man's links with God meet. The multiplicity of titles, most of them drawn on to the stage already in chapter 1, bears witness to this.

If Jesus has all this in him, then any contact with him is totally salvation-bearing. It is enough that 'we beheld his glory' (1.14), or, if it is too late for that, that we believe (20.29–31). The separate episodes of this gospel make this plain. In a way that is not found in the much briefer stories in the other gospels, many of them bring the encounter to a fully satisfactory theological conclusion: 'salvation' has in some sense been mediated when Jesus says to the Samaritan woman, 'I who speak to you am he' (4.26), or speaks similarly to the man born blind (9.36ff.); they need no more in heaven or earth. So for this writer, contact with the divine is contact with the divine, and that's the sum of it. He is intensely theistic, even when making Jesus the immediate agent for presenting God.

But he wrote a gospel, culminating in Jesus' death. This is not a case of adherence to a convention which was theologically redundant. 'Theophany' or 'christophany' is not the whole of John's concept; there is also movement. A film, with a dénouement, not a random set of slides. The death then primarily (though not exclusively, cf. 2.11) merits the term which most deeply expresses the presence of God's reality – glory (13.31f.). He concentrates, using every dramatic and literary device he can muster, upon the truth he wishes to communicate: that the splendour and reality of God are to be seen in Jesus' death and its circumstances.[21]

45

There is here both continuity and novelty. The death is of a piece with Jesus' eternal work; but it is nevertheless the consummation ('it is finished', 19.30) – and, theologically, there is no more to say. The central doctrinal picture is complete, and whatever follows is included for reasons which are, from this point of view, secondary. Thus, the resurrection is not the consummation or, as in Luke, the welcome reversal of a tragic death, but a demonstration of Jesus' essential physicality, the vehicle for a crucial lesson about faith (20.29), and perhaps for a few other, subordinate motifs.

Under (within might be better) the Spirit, the church lives utterly at one with Jesus, from whose inner being the Spirit came (20.22). As his wholly sufficient representative (14.25f.; 15.25f.), the Spirit will enable the church to preserve the state of affairs, characterized by mutual love (13.34), which Jesus established. There is ample joy in that, and, compared to its light, the vividness of the world's coming end fades. The Johannine picture of church life is static rather than dynamic, perhaps preservative rather than expansive. There is a total absence of Luke's feeling for the big, wide world: here, 'the world' is a theological term of the greatest moral ambiguity (see in chapter 17). It may be that both intellectual propensity and church situation impelled him this way. The Johannine epistles certainly indicate it.

These attempts to outline the theological patterns of some of the leading New Testament writers are given by way of samples. The same could be done for the rest. Some would enable us to exhibit an even wider and more surprising range of articulation of Christian experience. One or two seem in fact to be only marginally affected by distinctively Christian patterns of either experience or belief. As Luther saw, perhaps the Epistle of James particularly invites that judgment.

To point out this variety is no novelty. It is the current fashion of New Testament scholarship. We have done it with a further end in view: to see what it might signify when the doctrine-making mind is brought to bear on the material. That is, when we look at this varied evidence from the point of view of the traditional concerns of Christian belief. To what conclusions shall we be led concerning the nature of that belief and the legitimacy of the various possible ways of formulating it? How can we evaluate its clearly mobile quality amid the strong pressure to keep it static (or regard it as static)? Despite all its difficulties, is that pressure to be commended on other grounds? And looming always is the question: what is the status of the never ceasing labour to clothe Christian experience of God in intelligible words?

IV

The Doctrines

Traditionally and conventionally, Christian doctrine divides into topics which come in what seems a logically imposed order. There is teaching concerning God, man, the person of Christ and his work, the Spirit, the church, the sacraments, the end. And many of these subdivide: for example, the work of Christ into his life, death, resurrection, ascension and heavenly session. This classification, first visible in formulas which lie behind our creeds, and first appearing in embryo in extensive form in the work of Christian writers towards the end of the second century (Irenaeus, Tertullian, and Origen), was a wholly understandable development: he who reflects upon a tradition of belief must organize and systematize it, discover ways of bringing intellectual order.

But of course at the beginning it was not so. No New Testament writer worked to a pattern organized in this way, and we have no reason to suppose that any of them worked to it but concealed it, as a hidden programme. This does not mean that they thought chaotically. As we have seen, they had their own ways of ordering their belief; but when they created their writings, they happen, for various environmental reasons which we can go far to identify, not to have used that way. A passage like I Cor. 15.3ff. or Acts 2.22ff. is evidence of such sequential doctrinal thinking. But, however crucial in certain ways, it is rudimentary and never gets elaborated into anything like a treatise.) This means that when we look back at them with minds saturated in this pattern, the effect is generally to obscure their own patterns from our sight or else to distort them into more or less adequate attempts at dealing with the later and familiar agenda. We shall leave until the end an assessment of the effect of looking at them 'as they are' (an undertaking which in principle is not without hazard, cf. p. 15). Now we propose to see how certain of the familiar topics of doctrine fare at the hands of some of the New Testament writers. In passing, we may wonder how many of the headings would have been acknowledged by how many of the writers as workable topics at all.

But first we shall try to make our objective a little more precise. We shall be providing in this chapter sections which could bear titles like 'The Christology of the New Testament', 'The New Testament Doctrine of the Church', 'Atonement Doctrine in the New Testament'. There are many books bearing titles of this kind. We have already mentioned objections to such studies (p. 27 above). There are two chief ones. First, the title sets up a programme to which the writer is then constrained to work; but the programme itself makes assumptions which are open to challenge. Thus, in the case of 'The Christology of the New Testament', it is easy for a writer to feel, perhaps vaguely, as he approaches his work, the constraint of the developed subject, christology, with its range of topics, its set of issues to be dealt with, and its technical conventions. The enquiry then becomes: how is this package of ideas and questions evidenced in the New Testament? And the deflating question arises: what if those ideas are not represented in the New Testament and what if those questions did not occur to its writers? Even in the case of a scholar who is not so naive as to deny either possibility, it is easy to go some way along the path towards unwarranted hopes from the material, towards insisting that it yield results for which it was never designed and almost complaining when it fails to do so! A consequence is then that, in so far as he is moved in this direction, he is prevented from seeing what the documents are well able to disclose to him.

It is possible to overcome this objection by what looks like a simple verbal device. In fact it alters the tone of the study considerably and perhaps decisively. The programme should be not 'The Christology of the New Testament', but 'How does the New Testament think about Jesus?' The two starting-points seem close; the products may easily be very different. The second will have the advantages of being closer to 'ground level' conceptually (Jesus lived as flesh and blood, 'christology' is human talk about him) and of making interconnections with other aspects of the writers' thought smoother. Thus, while 'christology' and 'atonement' are separate doctrinal areas, each with its own history and conventions, 'thought about Jesus' opens easily into 'thought about restoration of relationship between God and man'. The variety of ways in which the two are linked in the New Testament gives the possibility of fresh ways of fiewing their relationship now. It loosens the structure.

The second objection to titles like 'The Christology of the New Testament' and even 'How does the New Testament think about Jesus?' is that they abstract artificially from the flow of a given writer's thought. Paul wrote Romans (for example) following a line of argument which to him at that time was compelling. To focus on certain passages within it, and set them alongside passages in other Pauline works, composed for other purposes at quite different times, and then to construct out of them a pattern labelled 'Paul's Doctrine of (e.g.) Creation' is merely to raise the question of the status of the work achieved. It is a conceptual fabrication. It corresponds to nothing that Paul ever wrote as a connected whole; it makes unsubstantiated assumptions about the consistency of his ideas through the passage of time; and it reckons upon the apostle's readiness to see his words torn from the context in which he placed them, as if it played no part in their understanding. Again, the New Testament scholar is often not so naive as to fall headlong into these threatening jaws. But every time he undertakes studies bearing titles such as we have mentioned, he walks, however tentatively, towards them.

And so in this chapter we look like falling into the trap! The difference (and our justification) lies in the purpose in mind. When we have done, we shall not suppose that we have produced results which are (leaving aside the question of intrinsic adequacy) significant in themselves. They will rather be investigations with an ulterior motive: to uncover, by one line of approach, the underlying skeleton of theology in the New Testament, in order to discover more clearly how it is made up and what its capacity is for clothing Christian experience in words.

CREATION

The exponent of the biblical doctrine of creation inevitably finds himself concentrating on the Old Testament.[22] The account he gives of the relative paucity of material in the New Testament depends on his approach. Some regard it as a testimony to the complementary quality of the two Testaments and to the necessity to balanced Christian theology of taking the whole sweep of divine revelation, first in Israel, then in Christ. But with whatever view we end up, we ought to begin by sticking to our historical last and enquire what was afoot in this matter in the minds of the New Testament writers themselves.

There is no denying that at that period the religious convictions which nowadays we put under the heading of the doctrine of creation were at a low ebb in the religious consciousness of many in the Mediterranean world. The Jews were no exception. Certainly, they did not fall into thorough dualism and deny God's creative power; but they were far from confident about the value of the created order which surrounded them and far from sure how closely God controlled its affairs. Seeing nature as the intimate disclosure of God's presence, valuing the world as dependent upon him, with consequent concern for those matters which, with novel technicality, we now call ecological or environmental; these interests were not theirs. Rather, they felt the force of that pessimism about the world of flesh and matter which came to its clearest expression in the following period in the teaching of the Gnostic sects, with the Manicheans as perhaps their most extreme example in this regard.

It is not surprising then that in the New Testament there is little sign of vitality of vision with regard to the material order. Not that there is anything like formal denial of God's responsibility as creator for the whole of the world. On the contrary it is affirmed: I Cor. 8.6; Acts 17.24ff. There are, however, tell-tale signs of pessimism: I John 2.15f.; 5.19. The world may have been created by God; but, effectively, that had become a 'dead' event, in the past, while present realities were assessed otherwise.

Nevertheless, in certain respects, the impact of Jesus seems to have had the effect of revitalizing belief in God as creator. In relation to the issue of what might be eaten and what might not, some early Christians took the logic of God's role as creator to be that everything could be freely taken as his gift: I Cor. 10.26; Mark 7.19; Acts 10.15; I Tim. 4.4. In the matter of marriage, Mark shows Jesus appealing to man's creation by God as the ground for life-long commitment (Mark 10.1ff.).

More deeply, it seemed appropriate to Paul, along one line of exploration of the significance of Jesus, to see the order which had derived from him as 'a new creation' (II Cor. 5.17; Gal. 6.15). So strongly was this felt that three writers (Paul, John and the writer of Hebrews) found it possible to put Jesus into the role occupied in Jewish theology by God's word or wisdom, as the agent of his creative work (I Cor. 1.24; 8.6; John 1.1–3; Hebrews 1.3). And Paul could foresee, as one dimension of that fulfilment which he expected God would soon accomplish, a rejuvenation of the whole creation: Rom. 8.19 (cf. Rev. 21.1).

The question is, What does this teaching signify? Does it represent a revival of vision with regard to the value of the created order or is its import (whatever its language may be) what we should now describe as firmly *other*-worldly? The latter may well be true of the Apocalypse of John, whose language in chapter 21 at first sight tells otherwise. Would it be truer to New Testament religious consciousness to say that, despite statements which speak of creation, the main object of attention is not 'creation' but 'salvation': that is, not with accepting, using and improving the world as God-given, but with seeking rest with God within and apart from it, if not in another 'world'? The fact is that much of the imaginative energy of the early church went into the expectation of the world's imminent end, and it is hard to combine that with deep appreciation of it as man's valued home.

With the qualifications which must be made, we conclude that the New Testament, left to itself, displays only a partial appreciation of those issues and interests which today command the deep concern of so many Christians in this area. Its writers are in the main more deeply concerned with issues which we can better describe as the rescue of man (or certain men) from the world than as their improvement within it. Despite certain moves in the opposite direction, there is in this matter a greater pessimism than the modern interest in the questions involved would be happy to share.

It is important to face this situation frankly if we are to understand the background to the present discussion over christology, brought into the open particularly by M. F. Wiles's *The Remaking of Christian Doctrine*.[23] Underlying that discussion and too rarely recognized is the dichotomy between the New Testament and modern religious sensibility on the question of God's relationship as creator with the world. Bluntly, the New Testament men, in terms of vitality of vision, made little of it; we are determined to make much of it. And the determination to make much of it is shared by many Christians, some of whom wish to stand by close adherence to traditional formulations of faith and others who are willing to move some distance away from them. The former inevitably feel that certain ways of emphasizing the role of God as creator undermine the traditional christology which they wish to maintain. The latter feel that justice can only be done to theism in present circumstances if christology takes a more modest shape. At all events, there seems to be an almost unavoidable see-saw effect: when the attention dwells upon God and the fullness of his activity, then Christ appears as his agent – a figure among others, however special and even unique in certain respects. But when the attention dwells upon Christ, and takes his divinity as a starting-point, with salvation as the dominant religious concern, then theism in practice recedes. It is hard for theological or religious sensibility at any time to give full weight to that which belongs to the areas of 'creation' and 'salvation' simultaneously. And there can be no doubt that christology assumed such centrality in early patterns of doctrine partly and precisely because hold on the underlying belief about the creative and sustaining role of God was imaginatively weak. At a time when that role assumes a more prominent place, it is almost inevitable that pressure should arise for christology to assume a different shape, with Jesus more as the expression of a God who is for ever and totally 'on the scene' than as himself a divine figure who once came to earth, sent by a God from 'behind the scenes'. And as far as doctrine about creation is concerned, whether the balance is redressed by recourse to the Old Testament or more simply to contemporary religious intuition – what is regarded as credible – is relatively a matter of indifference. The one may feed the other.

INCARNATION

'Incarnation' has become a quite ambiguous term in Christian doctrinal discussion. Sometimes it signifies the belief, formally stated in the classical documents of the patristic period, that in Jesus, godhead and manhood co-exist; or that God the Son, in the conception of Jesus, took to himself human nature; or, more mythologically expressed, that the Lord Jesus Christ 'came down from heaven and was incarnate by the Holy Ghost of the Virgin Mary and became man'. All these formulations involve the use of technical language, no longer current coin except in this context, but all of them come to this assertion: that in Jesus, God is personally known and uniquely present, living a human life. The intellectual difficulties are well-known and persistent: how can such a life be truly human, in such a way as to satisfy the firm claim of orthodoxy that so it is? How can the alleged uniqueness be reconciled with the omnipresence of God the creator, who identifies himself with all his creatures? How does God involve himself in the experience of *this* man but shield himself from the experience of the rest of his creation? How can God be uniquely incarnate in Jesus and also the kind of sustainer of the universe which such a God would surely be? The pressure of the difficulties is only intensified by the knowledge that in the intellectual circumstances of most of those who formulated the classical statements many of them were much less strongly felt; the demand of religious and theological sensibility that Jesus should be fully man was less intense than that he should be unambiguously divine. And the outlook of the times was frankly more mythological than many now find intellectually tolerable.

Nevertheless, the basic assertion seems to lie at the heart of Christian faith and arouses both wonder and the deep assent which wonder can command. It arouses too the sense that if *this* nexus between God and man is weakened, then certainly the distinctive glory has gone from Christian faith and perhaps the unique quality of the Christian hope has been lost.

It is true, however, that 'incarnation' is also commonly used to cover a wider and looser range of belief about Jesus: that in him, man that he was, we have a most particular, even uniquely precious, way to God. In this use, the nexus is retained, but 'uniqueness' is relaxed. (In fact, no orthodox doctrine takes uniqueness to the furthest point: the assertion of full humanity in Jesus goes a long way to prevent it.) That which binds Jesus to the rest of the human race is valued; he is seen in his place as a character on the stage of human history, one among the rest, but playing his own marvellous part. It is the inevitable bent of historically-minded man.

When we turn to the New Testament, we find that it matches neither the strict, patristic christology, nor the looser doctrine which, in one form or another, avoids the difficulties raised by the patristic pattern. To answer the question, Who was Jesus?, the New Testament writers work in neither of these idioms; and they differ among themselves.

We must shed one anachronistic impediment as we try to approach them on their own terms. It is common – but not allowable – to credit Paul, John and the writer to the Hebrews with a 'more advanced' christology than the other New Testament writers. The adjective often means that they come closest to later patristic orthodoxy, in particular that they assert the pre-existence of Christ: he was a heavenly being, uniquely related to the divine, who came to earth. But is 'advanced' not a very prejudiced metaphor, easily implying that higher marks are merited by those who occupy prematurely a position like that favoured later in the flow of time? If we leave it aside, at least we shall be prepared to see excellence of different kinds and let each say its piece.

In fact they are not without strong elements in common. They are united (apart from the Epistle of James) in giving to Jesus the central place in their work and their understanding of God. It is abundantly clear that as a result of experience of him, whether direct or indirect, that understanding has received a quite new character, colour and shape. Through and in him, all that they expected of God has reached (or approached) fruition. This is so much the case that in all the writings Jesus fills the foreground and God is, in a sense, taken for granted – while at the same time, the 'picture' of God implicit in the presentation is in process of receiving a new character. It is not surprising that readers of the New Testament sometimes emerge with a 'Jesus religion' rather than the rejuvenated theism which is in fact its underlying conviction.[24] But the question of his unique divinity and of what such a claim might mean is raised by none of them. Even when we read of pre-existence or that salvation is only possible through 'the name' of Jesus (Acts 4.12), we find no consideration of this question, no reasoning to lead us from these assertions to the claims inherent in the classical dogma, no argument excluding other possibilities. Pre-existence, with its background in Jewish usage for that which was supremely important as the channel of God's self-disclosure (e.g. the law), leads us by no clear and unambiguous route to the patristic teaching which grew out of it. Rather, it asserts the supreme religious importance of Jesus. And that claim is plain on almost every New Testament page – whatever idiom of expression is used.

Most of the writers do not use the 'advanced' ideas to which we have referred. Rather, Jesus is 'Messiah', or 'Son', or 'Son of Man'. Or else he behaves like a prophet of old, or teaches with a wisdom and authority outdoing the scribes. He is, that is to say, from many different starting-points, the one who opens up the way to God – as they variously conceived that way to be. We saw in the last chapter something of the range of interpretation given to him. We saw also that the writers' religious perspectives differed in what we, subjectively, are likely to call width and profundity. Our assessment of these qualities (like our assessment of what is 'advanced') is likely to be shaped by the theological tradition. But if we consider each writer's perspective in its own right, then within its terms Jesus is the agent of the transformation of outlook. So for Paul and John, his influence is as wide as the whole creation (II Cor. 5.17; John 1.1–18) and experience of him has affected the evaluation of everything; for the conceptuality of those writers had that width of range. In Luke this dimension receives little attention, but Jesus is the climax of 'sacred history' and, in a way that receives little intellectual exploration, is the centre of God's purposive action in human affairs. For Matthew, with his ideal of life as obedience to God's accredited teaching, Jesus is, not surprisingly, chiefly the messianic bearer of the perfect way.

What this amounts to is a conviction of the centrality of Jesus derived from experience of which he was the source. For an understanding of exactly how he gave rise to this extraordinarily powerful and richly diverse experience, the evidence for which lies before us in the writings, we are largely in the dark, though the gospels give pointers. The plain fact is that he did so. We can be sure, however, that in each case, the writer's circumstances and previous outlook have contributed to the way it was possible for him to receive Jesus' influence, whether direct or indirect. But still that influence was powerful enough to arouse the experience, so quickly and so diversely.

Such a theology might be best described as a transformed monotheism: belief in a God to whom Jesus has given colour, shape, and definition, and with whom the immensely creative impact of Jesus has opened up a new style of relationship. But it is important not to stress the diversity to the point of suggesting that 'Jesus' becomes vacuous – a label for whatever his followers chose to make of him. There is indeed a sense in which he was just that, and the history of the understanding of Jesus is littered with bizarre subjectivism: in effect, Jesus as the legitimation of all and any aspirations.[25] If that is what the New Testament accounts of Jesus amount to, then Christian history has amply taken their cue. But within and behind the diverse ways of expressing the experience derived from Jesus, the New Testament witnesses to certain dominant trends, worked out with varied thoroughness and direction. All found through him a new vision of God. It meant a new sense of the urgency of God's call and the immediacy of his power, a new awareness of gracious acceptance by him and solidarity with those of like mind, with a hitherto unfound freedom to give primacy to love, itself seen with new clarity to be rooted in God himself. All this was experienced as something that had arrived unbidden, God's gift. However its precise character, extent and significance were expressed, it was therefore seen as giving new vitality and direction to belief in God.

Whether it is just or useful to give to such a conviction the name 'incarnation' may be disputed. To do so may be a prime case of our prescribing the agenda for men who had every right to express their faith in their own way, and whose teaching does not in every case most naturally warrant that term, at least in its technical sense. It may also have the effect of constricting or confusing our own agenda, when, in trying to convey what Jesus means to us, we seek to clothe in words the rich experience which has derived from him.

RESURRECTION

One of the defects of the ordering of doctrine into a series of distinct topics is that the impression is easily given that they are homogeneous and capable of treatment along essentially similar lines. In general terms, the convention is to see each as involving a set of considerations, propositions, questions or issues (the balance varying according to the style of theologizing), which are discussed in terms of biblical or traditional material and abstract argument (again, the balance varying according to the theological style). This procedure obscures important aspects of the truth. There is a great deal of difference in the treatment they demand between those doctrinal areas which are speculative in character (e.g. the existence of God), those which involve an element of empirical observation (e.g. the doctrine of man), those where historical evidence is concerned (e.g. the person of Jesus, the resurrection), and those in which social as well as historical factors enter in (e.g. the church, Christian initiation, the ministry). Particularly in topics of this last kind, nebulous abstraction easily arises if the more concrete aspects of the question do not penetrate the doctrinal discussion. So, for example, an air of unreality is often given to talk about baptism when its alleged metaphysical nature and effects are so presented as to bear little clear relationship to the sociological setting in which we know and experience it.

In traditional presentation, incarnation and resurrection have been on much the same footing from the point of view of this classification. Each has been seen to involve the theoretical appreciation of historical circumstances, in the light of underlying theological assumptions of the first type we referred to above, the purely theoretical or speculative. Clearly, the resurrection has theological significance only on the basis of belief in God. Otherwise it can only be a wonderful, inexplicable or mythical occurrence.

In this context of belief, resurrection, as a theological topic, has always been bound up with the significance of the raising of Jesus from death, the 'Easter event'. Similarly, incarnation has been bound up with the story of his miraculous birth.[26] But, as we have seen, it is possible to consider that theological topic quite apart from any connection with this 'event'. So it has been for some time, a fact which may have helped to lead some towards a similar treatment of resur-

56

rection, as a theological topic apart from its traditional basis in an event. H. A. Williams's *True Resurrection*[27] is perhaps the best known example.

Meanwhile, scholarly discussion of the New Testament evidence concerning the subject continues to centre on the issue of historicity, generally by way of analysis of the theological motives to be discerned in the accounts given by the various writers.[28] But the issue is set in a theological light, and opinion divides along this line: if Jesus did not rise bodily from the dead, can there be any doctrinal content to resurrection? Does the theology depend upon 'solidity' in the event? How far is the renewal of vision or the conviction that 'life' is more 'final' than death and that God guarantees it – how far is this dependent on the historicity of Jesus' rising from the grave?

In this discussion it is easy to miss the fact that in the New Testament itself, the resurrection of Jesus has scarcely any connection with the areas of discussion which we have just surveyed. Among the New Testament writers, only Matthew makes an issue of the historicity of the event (27.62–6; 28.11–15) – and he may be thought to exploit the resurrection theologically less than any of the evangelists. He is simply out to rebut a Jewish slander and does not even show how the event fulfils prophecy, which was for him the sign of theological significance. Luke (24.37ff.) and John (20.24–9) both emphasize the firmly bodily nature of the risen Jesus; but they appear to be opposing a docetic or 'spiritual' interpretation of the resurrection rather than straight denial. And neither makes extensive theological use of Jesus' resurrection. Though it is true that resurrection as a theological area is central to John, in the sense that he sees God, and so Jesus, as giving 'life', he does little to connect the resurrection stories, by either verbal or thematic allusions, with this theme. It is the total mission of Jesus, evoking faith, which yields this effect (5.24). The story of the raising of Lazarus, with its climactic statement in 11.25, may be read as prefiguring the raising of Jesus, but it has to be admitted that John is remarkably reticent in linking the two, despite his usual skill at making such links if he wishes to do so. Paul, who makes more theologically of the resurrection than any other New Testament writer, is, paradoxically, the least explicit (among those who chiefly deal with it) concerning the nature of the 'event' itself. For him, it seems, the richness of meaning – and indeed the fact that Jesus had been raised – did not depend upon precision of historical knowledge at that point. That Jesus appeared to witnesses was, for him, of much greater significance (I Cor. 15.3ff.);

though he leaves us to guess what 'appeared' means.

If we distort the New Testament writers when we press them to focus upon the question of the historicity of Jesus' resurrection (and witness to our interests rather than theirs), the same is true when we look to them for material concerning resurrection as a theological topic. Strictly speaking, only Paul probes the theological meaning of resurrection and integrates it with the pattern of his mind (chiefly in I Cor. 15). He alone makes a considered theological scheme of the raising of Jesus and that of his followers and the relationship between them; though there are approaches to it in I Peter (1.3ff.) and the Revelation of John (21f.). From the Pastoral Epistles, we may cite the formula in II Tim. 2.11 ('If we have died with him, we shall also live with him'), which is reminiscent of Pauline language, but closer to the idiom of liturgy than of doctrinal reasoning; and the same writer in fact denies that present integration of Jesus' resurrection and that of the believers which is at the heart of Paul's teaching (II Tim. 2.18). Hebrews and the Johannine epistles make virtually no use of it.

The right inference is not that for such writers the resurrection was a false belief; no evidence points to that. Rather, for them it did not play a doctrinally significant role, and they found other means to express some of the convictions with which it has come to be linked. A resurrection is not the only way of connecting the earthly Jesus and the heavenly in the New Testament. Both Hebrews and the writer of the Pastoral Epistles, for example, are quite convinced of Jesus' heavenly triumph without making much of resurrection as the means by which he came to it after his earthly life. The Fourth Gospel sees a subtle relationship between Jesus' existence 'above' and 'below' which applies during the period of his sojourn in this world (cf. John 3.31; 8.23). It is his heavenly origin ('from above') as much as his heavenly destination which determines the effectiveness of his life-giving power, and his exaltation takes place on the cross (12.32). So 'resurrection' is not the only idiom for conceptualizing the vitality of God in relation to mankind and the assurance that the God we worship is, through and through, the life-giver. That faith has been launched in Jesus, and it stands – despite the variety of ways in which it was so soon apprehended.

THE MINISTRY

Some would argue that the ministry of the church is scarcely a theological topic at all. It is a matter of the church making the most suitable arrangements for its management. But along a number of different lines of thought it has traditionally been reckoned within the scope of theological discussion and formulation, sometimes to the extent of ignoring its organizational aspect and, as we have suggested, the effects of the historical settings in which the institution operates.

Most broadly, and now commonly, the ministry receives theological sense as coherent with the general sacramental nature of God's relationship with the world: he is to be encountered in persons, circumstances and institutions which are to be viewed in the light of their capacity to make him known. It is thus part of a general approach to experience which seeks to maximize its 'God-bearing' significance. There seems no reason to exclude the ministry from this approach, but, being general in nature, it is not calculated to yield what might be called 'hard' or technical theological results.[29] Still, it has the advantage of setting theology concerning the ministry in a wider doctrinal context.

Or else the subject is treated on the basis of the biblical material, as part of a policy of reliance on biblical authority. Such a procedure has to face at least three difficulties: a basic lack of information; a variety of practice in the New Testament period which can scarcely be eliminated; and the question how such institutions as can be identified in the New Testament may be identified and reproduced in the church of our quite different times.

Alternatively, tradition is taken as the relevant source of theological authority, in one of a number of possible senses. As indeed with the use of the Bible, reliance on the past may be at the level of mere practice: the institutions of the church in former times must be maintained. Because of the long continuity of the offices of bishop, presbyter and deacon, it is not surprising that this argument is used with special vigour by those Christian bodies which have maintained them. But a question is concealed by the continuity of names: how great is the continuity in what the offices have signifed in various ecclesiastical and social settings and in the tasks their holders have performed, and what difference does it make to the claim for continuity if the names have covered a wide range of phenomena in these areas? In other words, how much weight is it legitimate to place on the mere continuity of name and institution and perhaps of certain functions?

Or instead of the practice of the past, authority may be sought in the official doctrinal definitions of the church, statements concerning the manner in which the ministry is to be understood and received in the church. Or else doctrine on the ministry is elucidated in terms of rational deduction, against the background of particular philosophical assumptions. Each of these ways raises its own problems: the right of the church to define or the philosophical system concerned must be accepted before the doctrines derived from them can be accepted.

These methods of arriving at theology concerning the church's ministry are all alien to those visible in the New Testament writings. There the matter is never one of independent speculation or pronouncement, nor is it one of theological indifference. It is a natural by-product of more fundamental belief, or else the church's ordering is seen as part of the divine provision for its growth. So in the work of Paul, the apostolate is presented as reproducing the pattern of Christ, that is, with self-giving and suffering as the means of power and strength (II Cor. 4.5–12; 12.5–10; 13.4). Similarly, other functions within the congregation are seen as manifestations of the Spirit's powerful activity (I Cor. 12.1ff.). The ministry is understood along lines dictated by Paul's central theological convictions.

In Luke's work, we find that the ministry is an element in the providentially guided onward movement of the church and in the repeated pattern of promise and fulfilment. As we have seen (p. 41 above), the church's leaders imitate the actions of Jesus, in their own due time, as he himself imitated those of the Old Testament prophets. All occupy their proper place within the rhythm of God's actions in history. Also, the early leaders bear witness to the truth of the Christian message – they were there to see the happenings they proclaim (Acts 1.21f.). The phases of the action are thus bound together. We also find an element of response to new needs, when we read of the appointment of elders in newly founded congregations (Acts 14.23; cf. 15.6; 20.17). Here as in the Pastoral Epistles practical pressures are dominant. This is so much the case in the Pastor's work that theological reflection on the ministry is minimal, though the amount of space devoted to it is great (I Tim. 3 and 5; Titus 1.5ff.). For this writer, no doubt because of the situation in which he was placed, the overwhelming need was for leaders who would guard sound morals and orthodox faith, lest the church should crumble under the assaults of false and unworthy teachers.

Something similar emerges from the Johannine literature. If we are right in seeing the picture of the disciples in the Supper Discourses in John 13–17 as, at least in part, a reflection of the evangelist's conception of leadership in the church, then, once more, severely practical considerations have supervened when we move on to the situation mirrored in II and III John. In the gospel, the leaders' role is supremely the preservation of unity, expressed in the love which binds the Lord to his people and them to each other (13.34). They are, we may perhaps suppose, the route whereby the guidance of the Paraclete comes to the church, and in this too they perpetuate the work of Jesus (14.16–18; 16.15). In the gospel their disciplinary role comes to the surface only once: 20.23. But when the epistles were written, the tougher aspects of leadership are to the fore. The First Epistle of John shows that the ideal of love was being strained to breaking-point by schism arising, at least in part, from doctrinal differences (2.19ff.; 4.1–12). And in III John the situation is so serious that politics have banished theology altogether, as one leader vies with another.

The New Testament presents us with a picture of the church's emerging ministry which, at the institutional level, is not wholly clear. While titles and patterns appear to have differed somewhat from one place to another, there are common features. Fundamentally, the principle of ordered structure is accepted: there is variety of function and the exercise of supervision rather than flat egalitarian democracy. And there is strong pressure for the leaders to echo Jesus, by generosity and service – though this is lost sight of in later writings like the Pastoral Epistles. Beyond that, we must acknowledge variety. Not surprisingly, each writer reflects his dominant concerns. Those with the most powerful theological drive allow its dominant tendencies to shape their view of the role of the leaders, each in his own way; though it is to be noted that the Epistle to the Hebrews, with a highly developed theological outlook, is able to mention 'leaders' without theological comment of any kind – only their example is recommended (13.7, 17, 24). Practical pressures break in and their effect is to make it hard to maintain a theological vision of the ministry at all. But where it exists, it is intimately bound up with central convictions.

ESCHATOLOGY
In the New Testament, eschatology is not so much a doctrinal topic as a theological idiom. It is of course possible to define a theological area suitably labelled 'eschatology', and analyse the ample New Testament material bearing upon the theme. We may then classify the evidence; perhaps by subject (dividing it along the traditional lines into death, judgment, heaven and hell) or by general shape (whether the end is seen as close or distant, already somehow in train or lying in the future). But by neither of these methods shall we come

to the heart of what 'eschatology' signifies in the New Testament. The former prescribes an agenda which no New Testament writer saw in those terms. The latter fails to do justice to the place of eschatology in the overall thought of the writers.

It would be truer to their theological environment (in so far as it can be generalized) to see their christology, their attitude to resurrection and to the Spirit, as aspects of an eschatological world-view than to treat eschatology as a separate topic alongside them. To take a political parallel, it is not the most illuminating way of outlining the thought of a traditional Liberal to give an account of his thought about liberty alongside his ideas on trade, social security and defence. If he is a true Liberal, his liberty-loving cast of mind must first be understood for any of the rest to be intelligible.

For most Jews of the first century, theology was conceived in a predominantly eschatological mould. With the exception of the Epistle of James, this is true of the Judaism which lies, in different ways, in the background of the New Testament writers. That is, a primary truth about God, perhaps from man's practical point of view *the* primary truth, was that he would soon or one day act decisively in the world for judgment and salvation. It was this which saved Jewish theism from abstraction and gave the chance for God to emerge from pure transcendence. And it set a goal and purpose for the observance of the law which was in the meantime the expression of his will.

It was no wonder then that when some men experienced as a result of Jesus a decisive revolution in their relationship with God (and so with all else), by far their most natural idiom for articulating the change was the language and imagery of eschatology. For almost all of them this was far more congenial than, for example, a Platonist style of speech, which might have borne much of their sense, though it would have found it hard to accommodate the central experience of crisis and radical change. As the decisive irruption by God was 'present' or, quickly, 'past', whereas the language of eschatology concerned the future, a new use of the idiom was required. In the writers most deeply affected, the language and imagery of the future were transferred to the career of Jesus, from the realm of speculation to the realm of event, from fantasy expressing confidence in God to the interpretation of a known historical figure.

Or at least it was partly so: the process was not carried through rigorously, except, almost, by the Fourth Gospel. The onward drive of history continued. The conviction that in the future too God's action would persist could not so easily be dissociated from the eschatological conventions; so, often, the conditions associated with the end were seen as established in the world or in the church, but still awaiting their consummation. For the description of that, the old story stood its ground, with only necessary modifications. At that point, Christian thought coincided with its Jewish predecessor, except for the inclusion of Christian features – such as giving the central place in the final drama to Jesus and seeing the divine intervention in terms of his return. We may read the Revelation of John in this light.[30]

But the Fourth Gospel concentrates on what has happened in Jesus. It contains only a small number of statements which reflect the future expectation (especially 5.25–9; 6.39, 40, 44; 12.48), and scholarly opinion is divided about whether or not they are too firmly interwoven with the gospel as a whole to be taken as intrusions by an editor into the work as it was originally intended. In any case, this work goes furthest in seeing the old future hope as fulfilled in the coming of Jesus and the effect of that coming.

But how was this transfer of language and imagery achieved? The chief examples are these. First, the kingdom of God. The Old Testament and Judaism saw God as 'king' and his rule as one day to be established openly and clearly. The gospels show Jesus proclaiming this 'kingdom' as present in his words and deeds or else as following hard upon his heels: Mark 1.15; Matt. 12.28; Luke 11.20; 17.20f. Shed of its associations of magnificence and no longer on the grand scale, but retaining its association with general restoration and the defeat of God's enemies, the term is applied to what is, by the time of writing, the past episode of Jesus' ministry. But it retains its future application, especially in many of the parables which have it as their theme (e.g. in Matt. 25); and, as we might expect (cf. p. 39), Matthew sees it in an institutional light and sometimes seems to identify it with the church (13.38, 41). John, centering his theology on the person of Jesus, for whom 'king' is one of his titles (1.49; 12.13) and one way of expressing his belief in Jesus as Messiah (20.30f.), comes near to eliminating altogether a term which is dominant in the other gospels (cf. only 3.3, 5); though the idea of Jesus' kingdom as opposed to that represented by Pilate forms the axis of the trial scene in 18.33f. Paul, while, as we shall see, taking the lead in the great transfer of meaning which we are describing, does not do it consistently with 'kingdom of God' but uses it chiefly as a term for the future consummation, along more traditional lines (e.g. I Cor. 6.9f.; 15.50; Gal. 5.21).

The outpouring of the Spirit, believed to have departed from Israel as the last of the canonical prophets ceased, was longed for in the coming age, when its signs would be an unprecedented spiritual vitality and prophetic power among God's people. The prophecy of Joel 2.28 would be fulfilled. It is a measure of the vigour of the spiritual transformation of the first Christians that they found it natural to turn to this language to express their sense of what had happened to them as a result of Jesus – yet with the old world continuing its normal course around them. In Paul this awareness is palpably clear: I Cor. 12.1–13; Gal. 5.16–25. He is clear that the experience is intimately linked with Jesus and derives from him, though he fails to express the link with complete conceptual coherence (I Cor. 2.10–16; Rom. 8.1–11). The link with Jesus is also present in John's treatment: 14.16–18; 16.15; 20.22. Luke, with his broad historical treatment, is forced to show the new state of affairs within continuing ordinary human society; so miraculous manifestations come to the fore, above all the episode of Pentecost in Acts 2. But for him the Spirit was also the sign (very much in Old Testament style, cf. Judges 13.25; Num. 11.17ff.; Luke 1.15, 35, 67) of the authenticity of the first stirrings of God's ushering of Jesus into the world (Luke 1.35, 67).

Similarly, with the language of judgment. For the main New Testament writers who express themselves in the matter the future assize was a certainty (II Cor. 5.10; Matt. 25.31–46; II Tim. 4.1; Heb. 10.27; 12.23). Nevertheless, the most penetrating of them found it natural to speak of what had already occurred through Jesus as itself a judgment of God. Paul saw it as going only as far as believers: they had been acquitted at the bar of God, reconciled to him (Rom. 5.1; II Cor. 5.19). Given his acute sense of God's righteousness, he could express the sense of reconciliation with God in no other way. The future judgment was, in a sense, anticipated, its verdict assured: but II Cor. 5.10 shows that the old picture remained alongside. John, cooler and more reflective, sees Jesus' coming as in effect the judgment for all: 3.17–19. The language of the future event is brought wholly into the interpretation of the significance of Jesus.

The idea of resurrection faces us with a more taxing example. This too was part of the expectation of the end. We find it already in one of the earliest apocalyptic passages, Dan. 12.2. Yet it does not occupy so prominent a role in later Jewish apocalyptic speculation as to demand a place as of right in thought concerning the end.[31] Nevertheless, for some early Christians at least, it was part and parcel of their consciousness that as a result of Jesus the conditions of the new age had, in principle or in part, been anticipated and inaugurated among them. Paul expresses this sense of participation in resurrection life in connection with baptism, apparently taking its symbolism (entering water, then rising from it) as his cue: Rom. 6.3–11; Col. 2.12; 3.1. (And it seems that some took this in an extreme sense, II Tim. 2.18.) So in John, life in relation to Jesus who is 'the resurrection' (11.25) *is* already the life of the new age that, in traditional expectation, follows death and judgment (5.24) – 'eternal life'.

The other writers in the New Testament (except I Peter, at 1.3ff.) have not brought 'resurrection consciousness' into their sense of the new state of affairs brought about by Jesus. For them, the 'resurrection' of believers remains, as far as we can tell, something that lies in the future. In fact, we should use the word tentatively, for while they are sure of future fellowship with Jesus 'in the new age', we do not find the bridge between 'now' and 'then' expressed in terms of the believers' resurrection. Rather, they await the return of Jesus and see it in the context of an apocalyptic intervention described in terms which are basically those of Jewish speculation (cf. Mark 13; Matt. 24; Luke 21; Titus 2.13). For these writers, the resurrection of Jesus is an event, in the stream of events, asserting God's vindication of him, but affecting the believer only in the sense of placing him under Jesus' heavenly lordship and filling him with a sense of victory assured. But for Paul the believer's resurrection is integrated with that of Jesus (Rom. 8.11): the consciousness of a 'new world' is, in this aspect, linked with the 'event' of Jesus' rising.

We have surveyed what is perhaps the most creative theological undertaking visible in the New Testament. As we have seen, it was pursued with varying degrees of thoroughness by different writers. Those who took it furthest (Paul and the Gospel of John) came close to seeing 'salvation' or 'new life' as, in effect, that way of living with renewed vision, viewing all things afresh, which poets and contemplatives put before us; e.g. in Gerard Manley Hopkins' 'God's Grandeur' and Edwin Muir, 'Transfiguration'.[32] God had acted and all was new.

What had happened amounts to this: in order to find words to express their conviction that God had acted decisively through Jesus, these writers had to turn to the available stock of ideas and imagery for speaking of such things, the language of eschatology. But the conviction was the thing. Through Jesus and what had stemmed from him, they had experienced such a comprehensive revolution of life and outlook that no lesser conceptual steps would have sufficed. What they were not doing, however, is precisely what Christian theology has persistently taken them to be doing: providing information about last things. To suppose that was in fact to exploit their partial failure to take the full logic of the theological revolution upon which they had embarked (cf. pp. 62f).

THAT WHICH MAKES ALL THE DIFFERENCE

Atonement and salvation are both traditional topics in Christian theology. The former tends to centre on the interpretation of the death of Jesus, while the latter is more general, often concerned rather with the effects of Jesus' work as a whole. But neither quite comes to grips with the full picture presented by the New Testament. What the writers of those books join in giving is a witness to the fact that as a result of Jesus, seen as God's agent for this purpose, and as a result of what has stemmed from him, their relationship with God and their whole world outlook have been transformed. They are, however, not united in their account of what it was about Jesus that had made the difference or how the effect had been achieved. On that, they speak as their particular outlooks, circumstances and tendencies impelled them to speak.

We may put the matter thus: in the theological area usually designated 'atonement', the question to be answered, with regard to the New Testament writers, is not, What did they teach about Jesus' death? It is rather, What did they see as 'the thing about Jesus' which had 'made all the difference'? For example, if Matthew holds that it is impossible to enter the kingdom of heaven unless one displays a greater righteousness than the scribes and Pharisees (5.20), and if he is to be taken seriously, then clearly, as far as he is concerned, what has 'made all the difference' is Jesus' teaching concerning that righteousness rather than his death. But we must examine a range of cases.

As we saw in the last chapter, Paul thought that the cause of the transformation in his own relationship with God was the death-and-resurrection of Jesus. For the purposes of some of his images, the two are separated, though often they stand together as a single drama. He is led from his sense of reconciliation to God (II Cor. 5.19), which he knows to be the effect of Jesus, to interpret Jesus' significance in terms of sacrifice, which in his religious pattern was the way to effect reconciliation between man and God. No wonder then that he found

66

the source of his God-given peace in Jesus' death, that episode in his career to which the idea of sacrifice most obviously attached itself. Jesus' death then was for him a sacrifice offered to God (II Cor. 5.21) – though the 'shape' of the gospel, his sense that all came of God's free gift, compelled him to the paradoxical conclusion that (as in the classic case of Isaac and the ram in Gen.22) God himself had provided the offering by which reconciliation had been effected (Rom. 3.25; 8.32). But his sense of reconciliation is intertwined with a sense of victory – over spiritual powers, sin, the flesh, and all other obstacles between man and God. So participation in Jesus' resurrection is the key to a share in that victory (Rom. 6.9–11; Col. 2.12). Death and resurrection together sprout the foliage of appropriate imagery by which Paul can best express the transforming act performed by God in Jesus. There is no mystery in Paul's virtual ignoring of Jesus' life and concentrating on the final episode which is for him so fertile in vivid ideas that its historical basis virtually disappears from view.

There is no mystery either in the fact that other writers do not ignore that life: it is simply that they saw other elements as decisive for 'making all the difference'.

But it was the case with Mark, who first (as we suppose) set himself to tell the story which led up to the death, that he concentrated on it even more than Paul. His mind is far from being an open book (cf. pp. 36f.), but he seems to have told the story of Jesus' life largely as under the shadow of his death and as leading up to it, all part of a single contest against spiritual and human enemies. And, unless we are to read his resurrection story as in fact a foretaste of Jesus' return in glory, for him not far away, then we must confess that he does little to explore its theological meaning as a separate episode (cf. his 'you will see' in 13.26 and 14.62 about the return and in 16.7 about his risen presence). The death itself is interpreted as 'a ransom for many' (10.45), and the message to 'the many' is sombre: they will profit from that death only by themselves suffering like Jesus (8.34f.; 10.39).

For Matthew, the pattern is so different as to appear to come from a radically different kind of Christian setting. If we were to succumb to the impulse to take Paul as the norm of early Christian theology, then Matthew would have to be taken as a deviant. But for him too Jesus and that which has stemmed from him have 'made all the difference'. The death certainly plays its part: he retains Mark's saying about the 'ransom for many' (20.28) and virtually every word of his passion story. But that death is the solemn climax of the foreordained path he has to tread, leading to his glory, where he is with his people 'always, to the close of the age' (28.20). But if we ask what 'makes all the difference', then Matthew's answer is clear: it is Jesus' teaching, the content of the greater righteousness which gives the possibility of entry into the kingdom (5.20). To communicate this is the sum of the church's mission (28.19f.). His followers will adhere to it confident of his presence and happy in God's care (6.25ff.). Matthew's focus is on the pattern of Christian life, in its detailed obedience. Jesus' career is its foundation, the essential title-deeds; and for that reason the story had to be told and remembered.

Luke's Jesus is effective by virtue of the fact that his followers can enter the historical stream at whose centre he stands and whose true character he discloses. Life is transformed by being drawn into the sequence of promise and fulfilment whose consummation will one day come, at the end. Meanwhile, Jesus has 'made all the difference' at another, more detailed level – by the force of example. In teaching and conduct, by the manner of his life and of his death, he has demonstrated how his followers must conduct themselves; in generosity of heart, beyond all requirement (10.37), in open-hearted love (7.47; 15.11–32), in showing daily the self-sacrifice which Jesus showed in his final suffering (9.23). By planting this style of life, Jesus has transformed man's moral vision.

John, by contrast, takes us back to the relationship of the Father and Jesus. That relationship, stable and eternal (1.1; 10.30), is the foundation of Jesus' work. The work culminates in the cross, where God's true nature (his glory) is fully disclosed. But its effect is already portrayed in the Supper Discourses: the extension of the relationship to include the believers. They will share the divine unity (17.22), carry on the divine work (5.20; 14.12), abide in the divine love (15.10), and carry forward the divine mission (20.21). In every particular, the properties of the stable centre are shared out. The decisive factor is that Jesus came to make the sharing possible (1.14). John shows that in every deed of his life the new regime was established, and finally in his death from which flows the church's new, Spirit-led life (7.38f.; 19.30; 16.13–15).

In Hebrews, there is a mixture of the motifs we have found elsewhere. The writer has a mind theologically delighted with providential patterns fulfilled. So for him the proof that Jesus has transformed all things is that in him so many scriptural patterns are beautifully and ingeniously perfected. Taking passage after passage, as in a series of exercises, he makes the truth plain. This is at the level of word and intellect.[33] But this level of fulfilment gives straight on to another: as with Paul, Jesus' death is for him to be seen in terms of sacrifice. With his eye for scriptural detail, he exploits every parallel between the levitical law for sacrifices and that death, There is a sense in which here too it is the verbal fulfilment which for him 'does the trick' (cf. 9.22). But still, the event itself was required. Unlike Paul, who sees the parallel in terms of the traditional sin offering, this writer chooses instead, at least in his dominant pattern, the sacrifice of the Day of Atonement. He is thus enabled to unite the figures of the sacrificial victim and the high priest who takes its blood into the Holy of holies. Working out the parallel, he can then unite also, in a single process, Jesus' death and (not his resurrection so much as) his transition to heaven. There he presents the blood of his sacrificial death in the inner sanctuary of the universe (9.11f.). The chief feature of the transformation is forgiveness, the fruit of the Day of Atonement (9.14; 10.1ff.). The image itself determines this writer's emphasis on this effect of Jesus' work. No wonder that for him apostasy and relapse into sin are the greatest of problems: they deny the whole basis on which the new life rests, under Jesus' lordship and looking towards him (12.1–11; 6.4–6).

In examining our sample doctrinal areas (the range could be extended), we have found a variety of centres of gravity in the ways the New Testament writers expound who Jesus was and what he had done. They are united in proclaiming that as a result of him, that which concerned them most (however they defined it) had been quite transformed. Each reveals the basis of his religious concern: whether acceptance by the righteous God, or moral perfection from day to day, or an inner understanding of God's purposes. Few of them are wholly without any of these ingredients, but usually one predominates. In accordance with it, Jesus is portrayed in a certain light and certain lines of imagery are exploited rather than others. In the course of time, as the New Testament established itself as a unified canon and a norm of doctrine, the separate works were stirred into a mixture, the threads interwoven. So the individual colours were lost. The images, some almost poetic in their allusiveness, some used according to techniques established in Jewish scholarship, were turned into solid objects. The poetry was ignored, the techniques forgotten. So they became the building bricks for schemes of systematic doctrine. If we unravel, we may be able to free them to reveal the experience to which they first gave visual and verbal clothing. Our very gaze will of course distort them afresh; but at least we shall be looking, as the expression goes, where the action is.

V

Growth Well-rooted

It is time to sum up the conclusions to which this way of looking at the New Testament doctrinally (or doctrine New-Testamentally) leads. The most general conclusion is this: the logic of the doctrinal work of the New Testament writers seems to be that each of them, from his own standpoint, with his own intellectual and religious formation and his own special pressures of circumstance, applied to all necessary matters the implications of a theism shaped and defined as a result of Jesus. Each therefore worked within certain limitations of mind and setting and grasped certain opportunities which were open to him. Some seem to us more profound than others and some have generally seemed to be scarcely worthy to be called 'theological' at all. But these judgments are subjective and historically conditioned. We discern profundity of insight largely because certain of the writers have been so influential in later theological development or because they chime in to some degree with general philosophical assumptions which we happen to favour. This is particularly true of Paul and John. We fail to notice 'theology' in the case of Luke, for example, because we are accustomed to read stories for their narrative content and not ready to see them as the vehicle of faith. But all these writers wrote out of their faith: theology is implicit even if we have to adjust our sights in order to see it.

Each worked with a high degree of consistency. This claim needs modifying in the case of some of the writers who are dependent upon earlier models. They appear to follow them without always understanding them or perhaps agreeing with them. The Pastoral Epistles show signs of garbled Paulinism (cf. p. 34) and the Johannine epistles of garbled Johannism.[34] There is nothing surprising in this: these are among the first instances of Christian theology developing by using earlier authorities, and the art of accommodating old views to new is not easily acquired. But for the most part, the consistency is notable. With exceptions such as we have given from the later part of the New Testament period, the writers worked with a considerable degree of intellectual independence, unconstrained by instructions from on high aimed to standardize the articulation of faith. This gives them a sharpness of theological thrust. In the chosen idiom (if the idea of choice does not imply too great a self-consciousness), all matters deemed relevant are approached and dealt with, as part of the writer's uniform outlook.

The process was, we may suppose, largely intuitive: there was little awareness of successive theological problems needing to be solved by going through certain accredited procedures, at least as far as the central area of belief was concerned. In the Pauline epistles, it is true, we see the apostle at work on new problems, some theological, others ethical, and we can observe the authorities and the lines of thought which he found satisfactory. This is particularly apparent in I Corinthians. And the form critics have taught us to look for evidence of such work in the selection and framing of stories about Jesus in the gospels: the stories were included because they were found useful in giving his authority in matters where decision was now required.

But in all cases, the homogeneity within each writer's work remains impressive. If we attempt to identify the question implicit in the process of theological expression and application, we arrive (again, by another route, cf. p. 23) at the following: what are the implications of theism as defined through Jesus and that which has stemmed from him, for the area of reflection or practice under discussion? The consistency of the writers may then be attributed to their having held to this simple policy rigorously.

We advance the proposal that all good Christian theology should adopt the same method; with the qualification, now demanded, then only implicit, that it should be asked in awareness of the theologian's intellectual, cultural and ecclesiastical context, as providing both opportunity and limitation – lest he should regard his work as a last word (cf. p. 15). We do not propose this method just because we find it in the New Testament writers. For them there was little choice. The multiplicity of authorities arising from Christian history, with its controversies and its sheer length, was not there to help or hinder them. Their only substantial authority of the kind which Christians now find in Bible or tradition or magisterial documents was the Old Testament: it is significant that it is precisely in their rather artificial (as they seem) ways of using it that we feel them to be most 'odd'

71

theologically (cf. e.g. Matt. 2.23; I Cor. 9.9). When, as in their main theological thought, they are carried by the thrust of their Jesus-formed belief in God, then their supple creativity of mind is generally apparent.

They worked thus because it was natural for them to do so. We may imitate them because the method has recognized advantages. It makes for clean lines, for a capacity to follow a strong impulse of thought and produce clarity of message. It may act as a principle enabling order to be found in what often seems to be the morass of Christian ideas, words and idioms of thought, produced over so many years in so many different settings. It forges clear links between the basic gospel and its application to both theory and practice.

In the last chapter we glimpsed something of what this might mean in relation to certain areas of traditional doctrinal interest. But we now need to speak more plainly.

Christology comes first. For the New Testament writers, theism is a matter receiving hardly any treatment in its own right. God is as Jesus shows him to be, acts as Jesus acts on his behalf. At the same time theism is fundamental: the New Testament presents no 'Jesus-religion', cut adrift from God. If they seem to be saying that Jesus calls the tune, we read them wrongly: God tells Jesus what to play. But because the two interact so closely, christology needs to be attended to first. To understand it, we must ask of each of the writers: How does he understand Jesus? In what ways does Jesus shape and colour *his* theism?

For us too, if we have chosen to be Christian believers, it is (to state it at its most basic level) because we have come to find God, together with his creation and our relationship with both him and it, most illuminated by lines of thought which stem from Jesus, by one route or another. This sounds too cerebral, too cautious as a statement of fundamental Christian faith: it represents however the outline of its anatomy and may be accompanied by many different degrees and kinds of devotion, zeal and warmth. The skeleton of belief is theism given its colour by Jesus and that which stems from him. The christological question for us is therefore simply: what account of Jesus enables my theism to receive that Jesus-colouring? This question rather than, for example, What account can I give of traditional christological definition? To begin there is to begin too far above the root of faith, whether historically or in the pattern of belief. The men who made the definition were, after all, in their day working at our question in the way it was posed for them.

If we begin from the question recommended, then we shall be spared much unnecessary anxiety and methodological frustration. How much modern christology has reached an impasse through setting its task as re-stating the classical formulations of the fourth and fifth centuries and then finding it impossible to deal honestly with modern historical investigation of the gospels? It is no wonder that so little headway has been made in taking doctrinal account of the 'historical Jesus question', except in theology expressed in purely biblical terms, with its attendant disadvantage of archaism. There is no need for this frustration to persist. Let the results (such as they are) and the continuing discussion of the historical Jesus question be taken as scholarly methods demand. Whatever the findings, Christian belief in God stems from a complex of appreciation, evaluation and discrimination within which they form one element. That belief has no need to fear a situation where it is impossible to draw the line where knowledge of Jesus ends and early response to him begins. It has always been the case that Christian faith, not being a 'Jesus-religion', has rested not simply upon information about him, but upon witness to him by others. Greater awareness of the subtlety of the working of that witness, so that we see the mind of the interpreter at work in his seemingly most 'objective' reportings, alter the *shape* of the situation not one whit. Under these conditions, given by life in this world, we may seek to speak of Jesus. Not surprisingly, the traditional distinction, intelligible in older theological patterns, between the 'person' and 'work' of Jesus ceases to carry conviction. We know of him through his deeds and their effects. The conventional doctrinal topics of christology, incarnation, atonement, resurrection and ascension flow into a single whole. Christian belief is a form of response to Jesus as a complete historical phenomenon.

It involves also what we have several times referred to as 'that which stemmed from him'. From the start, Christian faith drew no sharp line between Jesus in the days of his flesh and his continuing effects in the church. Indeed, we now see how strongly the latter coloured the accounts of the former in the gospels. Those effects were spoken of in terms of the lordship of Christ or his indwelling of his people or the Spirit. In all cases, the language bears witness to the continuing dynamic power of his life and the refusal to see him as the mere repository of a teaching fixed for all time. Quite the reverse: in the first generation, movement and development were implicit, as I Corinthians amply illustrates. To be a Christian was not only to look back to him but also to swim in his wake. That wake, consisting of reflection on him and devotion to him, is inseparable from whatever we may mean by 'Jesus in himself'. Together they form the basis of the Christian style of belief in God. And the openness to renewed witness and fresh expression in new circumstances is, in principle, as available now as then. In that spirit, our doctrinal question about Jesus should be: What account of him enables my theism now to receive its Jesus-colouring?

As with christology and the areas which flow into it, so with doctrine concerning the church and the sacraments. How greatly ecumenical discussion might be eased if in the former area the question at issue were: What are the implications for Christian community of the style of belief in God to which Jesus has given rise? It would not produce immediate solutions of complex problems resulting from intractable historical situations. It would, however, have certain beneficial effects. It would, for example, enable the proper proportions and priorities of the problem to be maintained. Thus, a problem facing the church in relation to doctrine concerning itself is that of the weight to give to tokens of continuity. How important is it for the authenticity of the church that it should preserve continuously and intact authorities and institutions such as the creeds, the sacraments and the traditional form of ministry? The churches of the New Testament period neither envisaged nor considered the question. Biblical authority can give no explicit guidance. But the New Testament method may give a hint. Will not the question formulated above provide, not firm instructions, but at least a feeling for the manner in which the question should be handled? Clearly, it might seem, continuity in history has weight in evaluating manifestations of the Christian community; but the degree of weight would depend upon its place among a cluster of factors, and the touchstone might be the degree to which such continuity served to enable the basic understanding of God to be made clear. Tokens of continuity would stand not as qualifications which Christian churches should possess but as potential expressions of the gospel. By that test they would be judged.

The method is important negatively. Failure to use it has often had the effect not only of concealing more fundamental Christian faith but also of positively frustrating its purpose. Thus, it does not take much ingenuity to show that the proclamation of the love of God has sometimes been frustrated by insistence at all costs upon certain tenets of eucharistic doctrine or criteria of qualification for authentic 'churchness'. A non-controversial example would be the imposition upon England of an interdict by Pope Innocent III for several years during the reign of King John, so that the celebration of mass was forbidden, in deference to a doctrine of the papal power of appointing to episcopal sees. To us this seems an outwork of Christian theology, surely not worth such drastic defence. It seemed at the time by no means a matter of mere discipline; the area of doctrine concerned had its own validity and its own conclusions. Many examples lie closer to hand – and perhaps nearer the bone.

The recommended method may then have the effect of shifting the proportions within Christian doctrine, making questions which in another light seem vital to be matters of near indifference, or else shifting the terms upon which they should be judged. Some questions formerly seen as theological come instead to be matters of pastoral advisability or to raise issues chiefly of psychology or sociology. So it may be with the question of the best way of arranging procedures of Christian initiation, or in the matter of the ordination of women. So it may be also with questions of liturgical reform, so often discussed with a quite different range of considerations in mind.

To shift the proportions in this way often looks like abandoning the heritage of belief. Apart from overestimating the homogeneity and fixity of the heritage, that feeling fails to recognize the risks to the heritage at a deeper level if the proportions remain untouched. Anything which enables the basic thrust of Christian belief to be more clearly felt can only be gain in the present context.

This method also seems to be weak on revelation. Has not God through Christ and his church told us more than this? Is there not (to put it bluntly) more 'hard theology' than this in the Christian deposit? We have tried to show that in so far as theology comes in the form of human speech, there are certain important senses in which it cannot be 'hard' in the way we might wish (cf. pp. 15f.). But we have also tried to give a sense of the strength of the believer's sense of gift. He 'receives' God, he 'experiences' Jesus-and-that-which-stems-from-him. Theology arises only when he attempts to find words for these things. And then, with all due help, he must speak for himself in his own way. Words flow from persons, in particular settings of time and place and culture. They belong to earth not heaven.

Weak on revelation, perhaps, in a certain sense; but surely strong on 'Spirit'. That is, strong in showing the conditions in which theology can be the flexible response to experience in ever changing settings. The method can claim to substitute the supple freedom of David for the armour-impeded cumbersomeness of Goliath. The setting in which Christian theology needs now to be done (that is, in which Christian belief needs now to be rationally expressed) has changed in ways for which the David quality is certainly needed. For example, the fact that Christianity must express itself in relation to other equally sophisticated religions, themselves facing transplantation beyond their original homes, points to the desirability of more flexible and clarified ways of presenting it. Its distinctiveness should be seen at its true valuation and not exaggerated or distorted by failure to distinguish between the underlying Christian experience and particular hallowed or authoritative ways of expressing it. The aim should be to make it as easy as possible for common ground in theistic faith to be visible.

The fact that Christian faith lives now generally within a pluralist and non-authoritarian setting also points to the need for directness and simplicity as the condition for being understood. Again, nothing is to be gained by erecting high fences of technical language and thought-forms when the experience could be communicated, by way of appropriate styles of speech, without the need for such hurdling.

In so far as theology can turn to a greater directness of speech it will overcome another of its present ills. Except at the most trite or pietistic level, theologians have almost ceased to be able to hold together on the one hand recognizable Christian reflection and on the other the discussion of those areas of human life which lend themselves most obviously to religious awareness – death, love, moral sense, the formation of ideals. The conventional picture of Christian doctrine – of how dogma 'works' – goes a long way to forbid it. But once ask the question, What are the implications of Christian theism for an understanding of love (or death)? – and then two things occur: the right question is being asked, in an intelligible form, capable of leading to results which can be absorbed; and all relevant data, from many areas of study and thought, can flow freely into the discussion. It goes without saying that the same principles apply both to broad social and political issues and to more detailed ethical questions.[35]

The approach which we have recommended places the need for faith at one point only: belief in God as 'shaped' or 'coloured' by Jesus and what has derived from him. A man can set his hand to that plough or refuse it. Once he has set it, the rest is exploration – not a series of fresh, independent acts of faith. The exploration consists in attempts, in varied contexts, to express the implications of faith – as

Christians have always and diversely done. It is an approach to theology which not only seeks to use its resources intelligibly (to achieve that would be great gain!) but also to set store by two root principles of Christian awareness. It is as well to admit that they lie behind all that has been said. First, that life is to be lived 'by faith'; that is, by a rather special quality of light – which guides without dictating and assures without giving rise to complacency. Second, that idolatry is the root sin which ruins man's humanity as well as his sense of God, and that idolatry takes advantage of every chance to intrude.

Yet theology by its very nature always edges towards both knowledge of the unknowable and treating its own conclusions as final. Even as it forswears these objectives, it works to achieve them. The common instinct of religious people which leads them to treat theologians with suspicion has a good deal to commend it. For though religious people themselves, even when they do not seek to formulate their faith in rational concepts and orderly words, often fall into the same traps by other means, the religious aspirations of man are wider than theology is competent to express. Theology is the clothing of experience in rational words. The experience is of the love of God, his grace and his power, and it cannot be fully verbalized. The theologian's role is to speak clearly where speech is possible, and that opposition to his work which amounts to preferring obscurity where clarity may be had has nothing to be said for it. But he should know when to cease, and to define the boundaries of his competence is one of his tasks. If he goes beyond, he is guilty of reductionism: making all religious awareness fit the narrow bed of conceptual language.[36] There is more to religions than 'correct' speech about God; and if there were not, most of the speech would not be about anything of interest to us.

It is a common error (perhaps a piece of theological hubris) to pretend that religious language is undifferentiated; and such is the priority theology has established for itself (even when it is grumbled at), that it is often taken for granted that if it is to say anything worthwhile religious language ought to be theological language and conform to some version of its conventions. So liturgies go for theological 'correctness' – and fall flat. Not all religious experience can be verbalized at all, but much of it can be verbalized in terms other than those of theology. If only this were clear, people would feel freer to express themselves religiously in more appropriate terms. Some people see the point: which is why a fastidiously professional

77

philosopher of religion may like to worship in seventeenth-century forms and meditate on the writings of a fourteenth-century mystic. Words clothe religious experience in many different ways, appropriate to different facets of our sensibility. Our recommended theological method closes no doors on this. Indeed, it found its roots in the New Testament where the distinction between different kinds of religious language, along the lines we are now describing, is creatively blurred.

This study began from a sense of unreality in much that goes under the wide name of theology because certain close relatives (in particular, the study of the New Testament and the rational discussion of doctrine) seem to have moved into separate dwellings. But these two areas of study together illuminate the very bases of Christian belief. So the question arose: on what terms can they be brought into one house? Some of our present-day perspectives, derived chiefly from historical awareness, offered the possibility of interaction and mutual interpretation. The result has been to present a hopeful way forward which reaches out in many directions. If it helps to enhance the experience of God as a result of Jesus it will have achieved a significant aim.

And for myself?
The writer of a study such as this, which dwells upon the fluidity in a tradition of religious belief, invites questions concerning his own faith. Anyone who emphasizes the formative role of the cultural setting of religion, a setting which is continually on the move, cannot shelter anonymously behind 'unchanging tradition'. His work has an air of incompleteness if it does not offer some idea of his own way of clothing Christian experience of God in words. Not that his opinions are necessarily worth obtruding because they are his! But for two reasons the study demands the inclusion of at least a sketch of them. First, they provide an example of the process by which, in the play of circumstances upon that which has been received, theological formulation takes place, even when this process is far from being acknowledged. Second, they are not private opinions, but derive from thought and experience within the church, even if in certain ways they appear to diverge from traditional statement.

There is a streak in Christian tradition which holds that the incredibility of Christian affirmation, its capacity to amaze the intellect, tells strongly in its favour, or at least is something in which the

78

believer ought positively to rejoice.[37] But at a deeper (and tautologous) level, no one believes what is incredible to him; and if he takes on faith what he would otherwise find unbelievable, it is because he is predisposed to do so by some act of judgment or mental welcome.

We believe only what is credible to us. The conditions of credibility are provided largely by the cultural and social formation which we have undergone. We cannot be bludgeoned or shamed, and, on important matters, we can scarcely be persuaded, into finding credible what has not already seeped into our mental framework and permeated it.[38] That is why attack for heresy is always so unprofitable and why sudden conversion is frequently so shallow.

In the case of a Christian, that formation includes crucial Christian elements, though they are only part of it. It would take an impossibly intricate analysis to draw the boundary, for any individual, between them and the rest, drawn from the contemporary culture, and to show in what ways the Christian elements themselves and certain facets of the culture are intertwined. Inevitably, I do not believe as my fathers believed. Whether I find them attractive or repugnant, their words *come across* to me from an alien past, with which I can nevertheless feel a partial sympathy. I read Augustine of Hippo, for example, and feel moved partly to grasp his hand, partly to turn my back on him. Partly he excites and confirms my deepest convictions; partly he arouses such disgust that I do not wish to share a faith such as his. If I thus cleave Augustine in two, accepting this part of him and discarding that, I commit an act of macabre intellectual butchery. Better leave him whole and entire, in his setting, and better stay in my setting, whole and entire, feeling in no way compelled to entertain him but only that he is available for discriminating and appreciative encounter. I combine this with a sense of the transience of my own theological and religious judgments.

Bound in this complex relationship to the Christian past, in which partly I am deeply at home, partly a total alien, I am similarly bound to the world of my own time. My own formation at the hands of my (partly Christian, partly not) cultural setting leads me to adopt a position not only absorbent, but also detached, critical and creative. I produce my own, humble, variant in the contemporary pattern. It happens, not because I am in any way unusual in the possession of critical and creative faculties, but because reflection cannot work otherwise.

That which is decisive for me in my adherence to Christian faith

79

also affects many of my contemporaries. There are factors in our situation which throw into relief a certain quality of belief in God along the Christian path. These factors (deep assumptions about what 'must be') even mean for many that, if they are to believe in God at all, he must be seen as bearing this character. Otherwise, his existence is incredible; he is incapable of attracting adherence or worship, and it may be possible only to despise him. What is this character? I refer briefly to four features of it.

Firstly, he is a God of infinite compassion; otherwise his creation of so many beings whose lot demands such compassion would be intolerable in its callousness. As it is, compassionate love is the underpinning element in the moral life. Second, he so enters into human suffering and identifies himself with it that it is to be seen as part of the matrix in which good is made; otherwise, human suffering is an intolerable obstacle to credible theism; and, even on this account of it, strains it to the uttermost. As it is, losing life in order to gain it is the key by which we should interpret our lives. Third, human life and its environment are worth improving by all possible means; otherwise, God's role as creator is mocked or denigrated to the point of effective denial. As it is, we are to work to this end at whatever cost to our other ambitions. Fourth, God extracts from us a constant readiness to revise our judgments on persons and situations, relinquishing our settled values and standards; otherwise he would have capitulated to our concepts of him and the dimension of grace would be lost. As it is, we live expectantly for whatever the morrow will bring.

These four aspects of the divine character, compelling now to many Christians and colouring their Christian life, can all be traced to the foundations of Christian awareness in the New Testament. But they spring equally from the present sense of what 'must be', and owe their pressing quality to present circumstance. Indeed, it is not hard to show that in the form in which they now so strongly present themselves, they are not to be found in the New Testament. We may even be able to see that to be the case in the very moment that we find ourselves stirred to embrace them by the New Testament itself. Such an exercise of simultaneous detachment and appreciation may bring us, at least at an intuitive level, close to the heart of the interaction which is the subject of this study.

But for this to occur, we must see what is meant when we speak of their absence from the New Testament. First, the New Testament does not work out the meaning of God's compassion with the rigour which modern sensibility demands of God if he is to be credible or at any rate able to arouse loyalty. Sublimity of perception of God's love stays unreconciled in some writers more than others with a sense of his punitive, even vengeful judgment. Second, the New Testament indeed offers lines along which the 'problem of evil' can be fruitfully posed and alleviated – the image of the cross is the seed-bed of Christian thought to this end; but, as a 'problem' in the modern style (or even in the Old Testament style), it scarcely affects those writers. It was not out of our modern anguish, where it rocks the very foundations of credible theism, that they gave their doctrine. For reasons identifiable in their intellectual and religious setting, human sin was the object of much more urgent concern for them than human suffering. Third, the New Testament is not deeply concerned with the social and political improvement of the world. Quite apart from factors like the socially powerless condition of the church and its expectation of the world's speedy end, it was written at a time in the history of Judaism, and of general religious awareness, when hope and determination in that direction were particularly weak. That which is needed to impel such concern, a strong sense of the world as God's creation, was not then a point of vivid religious imagination (cf. pp. 49f.). And though the Fourth Gospel, with its proclamation of the Word's becoming flesh, has become the inspiration of Christian social reformers, it is very doubtful whether the writer of those words would have been other than astonished that such policies had arisen on the basis of them. Ostensibly derived from the teaching of that gospel, the inferences come in fact from a much wider range of convictions, some of them lying in the even deeper roots of Christian faith (e.g. concerning the creative love of God). Finally, the New Testament does not itself show awareness of that element of scepticism concerning all human evaluations and concepts, even ideas concerning God and his will, to which, by oblique inspiration, it no doubt prompts us. Quite the contrary, it reflects an assurance among the first Christians about themselves, their destiny and their teaching, whose mood the modern anti-idolater, who wishes to live by faith, finds it hard to share in this respect. For them, God's act of upturning values and expectations had taken place, in the past, in Jesus; for him, on the other hand, that 'living by faith' by which he swears lies at a different level, conditioned by quite different and much more recent influences. It is a way of reacting to all the ordinary contingencies and vicissitudes of life, as it plays out its course.

My way of experiencing God and clothing that experience in words is then along a path initiated by Jesus, with the impulse given by the New Testament, but it is related to him and it in a way formed by what in the world demands my belief and adherence. The result may sometimes be, in relation to the New Testament, to bring out a latent logic, sometimes to contradict, and, if to embrace, then still with an awareness of how alien it is even in the very moment of its intense attractiveness. For, yes indeed, by whatever route and with whatever adaptation, the pattern of my response to God arose from those writings and could never have been formed without them. In each aspect of it, I can both see the source and trace the route by which, in its own new shape, it reaches me and my contemporaries. I also know the gap which divides me from those who are unaffected by it, and regard their lack of it as sad impoverishment.

This discussion has all been related to the orderly verbal expression of belief. So we repeat, in this more personal context, what has already been said: that this level of expression ought not to stand alone. It is nourished by other expressions of that belief, both verbal and non-verbal; and it serves them by checking them. Those expressions are much more individual; so that any man's recital of that which nourishes him may arouse few comprehending or sympathetic echoes even among those who know him well. At this level, culture fragments. The composition of the list and its mode of operation will probably mystify even the man who draws it up. It will consist of scripture, liturgy, poetry, art, music; their conceptual links with his articulate thought may be obscure, subterranean, and sometimes quite absent. In my case, I doubt whether it would include the work of many theologians – apart from him to the memory of whose special gift in this regard this study is therefore dedicated.

Notes

1. J. L. Houlden, 'Liturgy and her companions,', in *The Eucharist Today*, ed. R. C. D. Jasper, SPCK 1974.

2. See Wolfhart Pannenberg, *Jesus – God and Man*, SCM Press 1968.

3. See Jürgen Moltmann, *Theology of Hope*, SCM Press 1967.

4. The reader of D. G. Rowell, *Hell and the Victorians*, Oxford University Press 1974, including the reader who thinks of himself as traditional and unadventurous in his religious convictions, will find himself in a world of sensibility which he simply cannot share – yet in the intervening period no reformulations of official belief on the subject have taken place. A major revolution has occurred in this crucial area of belief, but its implications seem not to have been absorbed by the great majority of those affirming adherence to fully orthodox faith.

5. For expressions of this conviction in a wide range of Christian theologians, see *Words About God*, ed. I. T. Ramsey, SCM Press 1971.

6. See further: Owen Chadwick, *From Bossuet to Newman*, Cambridge University Press 1957; J. L. Houlden, 'The Bible and the Faith' in *Catholic Anglicans Today*, ed. J. Wilkinson, Darton, Longman & Todd 1968; D. Nicholls, 'Modifications and Movements', *Journal of Theological Studies*, new series, 25, 1974; Keith Thomas, *Religion and the Decline of Magic*, Penguin Books 1971; D. Cupitt, *The Leap of Reason*, SPCK 1976.

7. For the story of this aspect of gospel scholarship, see W. R. Farmer, *The Synoptic Problem*, Macmillan, London and New York 1964, chs I–IV, and for one modern attempt to disturb the 'agreed solution', see ch. VI of the same work.

8. For an early essay in this direction, see A. M. Farrer, 'On dispensing with Q', in *Studies in the Gospels*, ed. D. E. Nineham, Blackwell 1955; and for more recent and thoroughgoing studies, see M. D. Goulder, *Midrash and Lection in Matthew*, SPCK 1974, and J. Drury, *Tradition and Design in Luke's Gospel*, Darton, Longman & Todd 1976.

9. See F. C. Grant, *The Gospels*, Faber & Faber 1959, pp. 52ff.; M. D. Hooker, 'On Using the Wrong Tool', in *Theology*, Vol. 75, 1972, pp. 570ff.

10. Rudolf Bultmann, *The History of the Synoptic Tradition*, ET, Blackwell 1963, but originally published in German in 1921.

11. Some of the leading studies in this field are: for Matthew, G. Bornkamm, G. Barth and H. J. Held, *Tradition and Interpretation in Matthew*, ET, SCM Press 1963; M. D. Goulder, *Midrash and Lection in Matthew*; for Mark, W. Marxsen, *Mark the Evangelist*, ET, Abingdon, New York 1969; E. Trocmé, *The Formation of the Gospel According to Mark*, ET, SPCK 1975; for Luke, H. Conzelmann, *Theology of Luke*, ET, Faber & Faber 1960; *Studies in Luke–Acts*, ed. L. Keck and J. L. Martyn, SPCK

1968; E. Franklin, *Christ the Lord*, SPCK 1975; for John, B. Lindars, *Behind the Fourth Gospel*, SPCK 1971; J. L. Martyn, *History and Theology in the Fourth Gospel*, New York 1968. And for a general account, see J. Rohde, *Rediscovering the Teaching of the Evangelists*, SCM Press 1968.

12. For an example of its application to the Revelation of John see P. Minear, 'The Cosmology of the Apocalypse' in *Current Issues in New Testament Interpretation*, ed. W. Klassen and G. F. Snyder, SCM Press 1962; and for an attempt to bring the Johannine Epistles more closely within the orbit of work achieved on The Gospel of John, see the present writer's *The Johannine Epistles*, A. & C. Black 1974.

13. Contrast for example in relation to the miracle stories in the gospels, the treatment given in A. Richardson, *The Miracle Stories of the Gospels*, SCM Press 1941, and J. M. Hull, *Hellenistic Magic and the Synoptic Tradition*, SCM Press 1974, the former 'homogenizing' what the latter analyses; and for the parables, on the one hand J. Jeremias, *The Parables of Jesus*, ET, SCM Press 1954, and on the other hand M. D. Goulder, 'Characteristics of the Parables' in *Journal of Theological Studies*, new series, 19, 1968, pp. 51–70.

14. But contrast the uncomplicated and simply approving attitude to law shown in I Tim. 1.8ff. with the subtle and tortuous teaching of Paul on the subject.

15. It is probable that lines 1, 4 and 5 represent his action on earth, the rest the heavenly acclaim accorded to him. See E. Schweizer, 'Two New Testament Creeds Compared' in *Current Issues in New Testament Interpretation*, and J. D. G. Dunn, 'Jesus – Flesh and Spirit', in *Journal of Theological Studies*, new series, 24, 1973, p. 63.

16. On the former point, contrast Mark 8.21 and its parallel Matt. 16.12 and cf. 13.51; on the latter, notice the omission of the details in Mark 7.33 in the Matthean parallel at 15.29–31 – among numerous examples, cf. J. M. Hull, op. cit., ch.VII.

17. For the former, see 27.24f., and the latter, 27.51–3 and 27. 62–6; 28. 11–15.

18. For Stephen, it is brought out most strikingly in utterances; compare Acts 7.55 with Luke 22.69; Acts 7.59 with Luke 23.46; and Acts 7.60 with Acts 23.34. For Peter, it is in features of the story; Peter in prison at Passover time between two guards, as Jesus suffered between two thieves; the angelic intervention when he is 'raised', and his being taken for a ghost, as, in Luke, the risen Jesus was (Luke 24.37). For Paul, in aspects of the trials, most clearly in the fact that both he and Jesus (in Luke's gospel alone) are brought before a Herod (Acts 26 and Luke 23.6ff.).

19. Perhaps the source of the rules in Acts 15.20 is the terms given in Deut. 12 for life in the Promised Land; cf. J. L. Houlden, *Ethics in the New Testament*, Penguin Books 1973, and Mowbray 1975, p. 61; J. C. O'Neill, *Theology of Acts*, SPCK 1970; M. Simon, 'The Apostolic Decree and its Setting in the Ancient Church', *Bulletin of the John Rylands Library*, 52, 1970, pp. 437ff.

20. See E. Käsemann, *The Testament of Jesus*, SCM Press 1968, which may be thought to generalize too much from John 17 with which it is primarily concerned. That chapter conveys the sense of salvation as a haven more powerfully than any other part of the gospel.

21. E.g. the elaboration of the Jesus–Pilate (God–World) confrontation in chs 18–19, so as to raise the question, Who is judging whom? Also, the ambiguous use of words like 'lift up', 12.32, meaning the lifting up in crucifixion and the exaltation in divine triumph. See J. C. Fenton, *The Passion According to John*, SPCK 1961; B. Lindars, *The Gospel According to John*, New Century Bible, Oliphants 1972.

22. For a recent example, see J. A. Baker, 'Biblical Attitudes to Nature' in *Man and Nature*, ed. H. Montefiore, Collins 1975.

23. M. F. Wiles, *The Remaking of Christian Doctrine*, SCM Press 1974.

24. See J. L. Houlden, 'The Place of Jesus', in *What About the New Testament?*, ed. C. A. Hickling and M. D. Hooker, SCM Press 1975.

25. See H. J. Cadbury, *The Peril of Modernizing Jesus*, SPCK 1962.

26. In the preceding section we refrained from treating the topic in these terms because we wanted to examine it more generally in the setting of its New Testament expression: we were concerned with 'what they thought of Jesus'. In fact, belief in a miraculous birth of Jesus, evidenced only in the gospels of Matthew and Luke, and playing a different role in each, does not entail belief in the 'incarnation' of God in Jesus, nor does this belief entail belief in his miraculous birth (as the fact that the Fourth Gospel, coming closest to a strictly incarnational account, fails to include it in its doctrinal structure, plainly indicates). For an account of the quite diverse doctrinal interpretations given to the story of Jesus' conception in the New Testament and the early church, see H. von Campenhausen, *The Virgin Birth in the Theology of the Ancient Church*, SCM Press 1964.

27. H. A. Williams, *True Resurrection*, Mitchell Beazley 1972.

28. See W. Marxsen, *The Resurrection of Jesus of Nazareth*, ET, SCM Press 1970; C. F. Evans, *Resurrection in the New Testament*, SCM Press 1972; D. Cupitt, *Christ and the Hiddenness of God*, Lutterworth 1971, ch. 10; also correspondence between C. F. D. Moule and D. Cupitt in *Theology*, 75, 1972.

29. For an eloquent example of the sacramental approach to this subject, see the sermon 'Walking Sacraments' in A. Farrer, *Celebration of Faith*, Hodder & Stoughton 1970.

30. Though more subtle views may be taken of it. For discussion of its theological stance, see G. B. Caird, *The Revelation of St John the Divine*, A. & C. Black 1966, pp. 289ff.; P. S. Minear, 'The Cosmology of the Apocalypse', in *Current Issues in New Testament Interpretation*, pp. 23ff.

31. See C. F. Evans, op. cit., ch. 1.

32. Gerard Manley Hopkins, 'God's Grandeur', *Collected Poems*, Oxford University Press 1948, p. 70, 1970 edition, p. 66; Edwin Muir, 'Transfiguration', *Collected Poems*, Faber & Faber 1960, p. 198.

33. His chief passages are Ps. 8. 4–6, in 2. 6–8; Ps. 95. 7–11, in 3. 7–11; Ps. 110. 4, first in 5.6; Jer. 31. 31–34, in 8. 8–12; and Ps. 40. 6–8, in 10. 5–7.

34. Cf. J. L. Houlden, *The Johannine Epistles*, A. & C. Black 1973, pp. 13f.; 19f. Our statement takes Paul's genuine epistles and the Gospel of John as norms.

35. Cf. J. L. Houlden, *Ethics and the New Testament*, Penguin Books 1973 and Mowbray 1975; G. R. Dunstan, *The Artifice of Ethics*, SCM Press 1974.

36. See Richard Spilsbury, *Providence Lost*, Oxford University Press 1974, especially ch. 3.

37. A notion generally fathered, apparently unjustly, on Tertullian; cf. T. D. Barnes, *Tertullian*, Oxford University Press 1971, pp. 223f.

38. Apart, that is, from the use of exceptional techniques to impose pressure; even then, deeply held belief often survives.

Index of Names and Topics